WHAT PEOPLE ARE SAYING

Your people are your most important asset and the engine that keeps an organization running. Building great teams who share your mission, vision, and values is essential when driving and thriving, especially in difficult times. One clogged artery, or someone who doesn't share that vision, can prove deadly. A leader's role is to empower their people to evangelize the organization and Dawn's book provides 6 key elements that determine whether you'll either need CPR or an undertaker.

—JEFFREY HAYZLETT
Primetime TV & Podcast Host, Speaker,
Author and Part-Time Cowboy

Heartbeat Leadership perfectly exemplifies the purpose and values that guide Dawn Kirk in all she does and who she is as a person and a leader. Whether you are new to leadership or a seasoned veteran, the insights and experiences throughout Heartbeat Leadership apply in pursuit of your best self!

—GLEN WALTER,
President North America, Mondelēz International

My good friend Dawn Kirk has put together a remarkable book. But the best part of this book is she spent decades living it. This is not just theory. This is like Michael Jordan writing a book about basketball; you'd better believe she knows what she's talking about. Her results speak for themselves. Simply put, this book will change your leadership and your life!

—LEE ALLEN JENKINS,
Pastor & Author, Eagles Nest Church

This book is a must read for all leaders who want to raise performance and nurture the heart of the organization at the same time—it's people. Many organizations talk about a "people-first approach" to their business, but their actions speak only to financial results. Heartbeat Leadership is a simple, effective playbook that follows "Six Pulses" to empower leaders, guide them to better engagement with their teams, and make a stronger impact on the organization.

—DENNIS ADAMOVICH,
Former CEO-College Football Hall of Fame

Dawn Kirk's book *Heartbeat Leadership* is a smart, evidence-based work on leadership in this era. It is based on lessons learned from her years in corporate America where she implemented many of the exact strategies to bring out the best in people. It is a must-read for anyone looking to take their leadership to the next level in the most productive way.

—JEFF SHEEHAN,
President, Sheehan Marketing Strategies

There are many people who talk about how to be a more effective leader, but in *Heartbeat Leadership* Dawn Kirk outlines a simple, yet profound approach, backed by modern research, to achieve more by putting people first.

—TERI P MCCLURE,
*General Counsel and Chief Human Resources
Officer for UPS (retired)*

Dawn provides a best-in-class perspective on excelling as a Fortune 50 executive in *Heartbeat Leadership*. She strikes an unprecedented balance of theory and practice applicable regardless of your position in the marketplace. Her unique style and people-centered approach challenges conventional thinking yet positions you for sustained growth in your life and career.

—**ANTHONY FLYNN,**
Founder/Amazing CEO

Some leaders inspire ambition without results. Some improve results but ignore the spirit. In *Heartbeat Leadership*, Dawn Kirk advocates for the rare, third type of leadership, one that raises performance and nurtures the heart of the company—it's people.

—**JACQUELINE M. WALTERS,**
M.D Comprehensive Women's OB/GYN, Managing Partner;
Owner, JMW Entertainment

HEARTBEAT LEADERSHIP

Empower Yourself
Engage Your Team
Impact Your Organization

DAWN S. KIRK

PRESS

To my Lord and Savior, Jesus Christ.
I give you all the honor, glory, and praise.

To my parents, Roy and Patricia Johnson, who taught me I can achieve anything if I was willing to put in the work and who invested in all of my dreams.

To my sister Dorian Johnson who moved to be my nanny through one of the most difficult career transitions of my life.

To my husband Tony and children Kendall and Kristopher for loving and supporting me in all of my endeavors.

CONTENTS

INTRODUCTION

One of my favorite quotations is this: "It's not what happens to you, but how you react to it that matters." (Epictetus) I was originally scheduled to launch my book in April 2020 when the COVID-19 pandemic hit in early March. I would have never guessed that we would face a pandemic of this magnitude in our lifetimes. My focus shifted from completing this book to ensuring my family and I were adjusting to our new norms—teenagers at home all day, my sister working her call center job from home, transitioning my business, my networking organization, and working with my church to adjust to virtual. Preparing for sheltering in place left little room for completing my book. After all, I would not be able to promote my book as planned, and marketing my book just didn't feel like the right thing to do during that time.

But as demand for my executive coaching services grew during this time, I saw firsthand the impact COVID-19 was having in the workplace. I quickly realized I had to finish this book because people were more important now than ever. During times like this, people who value people are desperately needed.

This book is now even more relevant because people are truly at the heart of this pandemic that has simultaneously impacted every individual, leader, and organization. As an individual, you have to figure out how to empower yourself to navigate this crisis personally and professionally. As a leader, you have to solve the problem of how to keep your team engaged. Organizations have to figure out how to continue to deliver profitable results.

The answers to all of these complex problems lie within the heart of your organization—PEOPLE. In this book, I will share with you the 6 Pulses to empower you, engage your team, and impact your organization. These Pulses stand the test of time—and pandemics. I know from experience these principles work. I believe strongly that implementing these Pulses will make all the difference in your personal, profession, and organizational recovery from this pandemic.

More than ever, people are the heartbeat of business!

—Dawn S. Kirk

CHAPTER 1

THE HEARTBEAT OF BUSINESS

T*hump-thump. Thump-thump.*

Do me a favor. Put your fingers up to your neck right now, just to the left or right of your throat. Do you feel it?

Thump-thump. Thump-thump.

You don't need a medical degree to recognize the consistent, steady beat of your heart.

Thump-thump. Thump-thump.

It's been working 9-5, graveyard shift, and overtime your entire life, about 100,000 beats a day, without you ever having to think about it.

Thump-thump. Thump-thump.

With each pulse, it pushes oxygenated blood through a network of arteries, veins, and capillaries that, if laid end to end, would stretch more than 60,000 miles!

But this is one muscle we easily take for granted because we don't see it at work. Biceps, glutes, abs—we'll pour hours and hard-earned dollars into getting results with those, but it's all too easy to neglect the heart. After all, it just keeps on ticking....

That is, until a tingling sensation begins in your arm. Shooting pain grips your chest. By the time you're faced with the painful consequences of a heart problem, it's usually too late to change course.

Today, the heart makes the news more often. Smartwatches and Fitbits track heart rates and count daily steps. Restaurant menus display encouraging little *heart-healthy* symbols. Unfortunately, ironically and tragically, heart disease is still both a leading cause of death and one of the most preventable. Everyone knows their heart should be cared for through diet and exercise. *But* we don't give the heart the attention it needs.

Genetics and environment will always play a part, but the greatest contributors to heart health are the lifestyle choices we make. It's a domino effect of small, heart-healthy habits. When you take care of the heart, you take care of the entire body.

> JUST AS THE HEART IS CENTRAL TO THE FUNCTIONING OF THE BODY, PEOPLE ARE THE HEART OF YOUR ORGANIZATION. THEY ARE THE BAROMETER TO INDICATE HOW WELL IT IS FUNCTIONING.

Now you might be saying, *Dawn, that's a nice biology lesson, but I thought this was a book about leadership.*

You're right. Just as the heart is central to the functioning of the body, people are the heart of your organization. They are the barometer to indicate how well it is functioning. Are you heart healthy? As a leader, are you in the early stages of congestive heart failure, or do you need a defibrillator? What's your pulse? What's the pulse of your team? What's the pulse of your organization?

It's time for a heart check.

BUSINESS BIOLOGY 101

I've seen it proved time and time again; every organization is a living body, driven by an "organ" just as critical to life as your heart. It, too, has a pulse—a heartbeat—that pumps energy throughout the organization and positions it to achieve results.

Unlike your involuntary *thump-thump, thump-thump,* an organization's heartbeat is a little more complex. It requires intentional care. It won't run on fumes forever. It will even walk right out of the office if it's taken for granted. It requires leadership that *gets it,* that understands the business biology of an organization.

What is the heartbeat of every organization? *People.*

Sadly, most organizations have a heart problem, *and they don't even know it.* They're like the great-uncle who gorges on unhealthy food, never exercises, and then suddenly feels a horrible chest pain. At that point, panic sets in, stress skyrockets, and everyone runs around yelling, "How did *this* happen?!"

Sound familiar? As a leader in large corporations for over twenty-five years, I have felt these pains all too well and seen so many people exasperated by them. As one of the few African-American women accepted into the Manager Training Program at Frito-Lay Inc., I was determined to smash through the glass ceiling and grab my corner office in the sky. To say I was driven to succeed would be an understatement. What I discovered is that the glass can feel a lot more like cold, impenetrable steel, especially when companies focus more on hard numbers and neglect the beating hearts that makes it possible to achieve results.

Numbers may be easier to see, but failing to put people first actually cripples any organization's ability to get stellar results consistently. Not that companies don't talk the right game when it comes to people. However, let's face it—it's easy to say you are *people-first*, but it's much harder to put into practice. Stats and quarterly reports are easier to read than a frustrated middle manager—and numbers don't get their feelings hurt. On the one hand, it's understandable. After all, businesses exist to make money. No money, no business.

> ACROSS INDUSTRIES, LOCATIONS, JOB TITLES, OR OUTCOMES, ONE THING REMAINS TRUE: PEOPLE ARE THE HEARTBEAT OF BUSINESS.

But it's also fair to say *no people, no business.* Across industries, locations, job titles, or outcomes, one thing remains true: people are the heartbeat of business.

Why? It may help to think about it this way:

- *People are innovators.* They look for ways to make things better for customers.

- *People have heart.* They buy into an organization because it represents something larger than themselves.

- *People influence other people.* They bring out the best in their teams and all levels of the organization.

- *People develop better processes.* They are on the front lines looking for ways to improve, innovate, and execute.

- *People are more than the sum of their parts.* They join with other people to do more than they could alone and go farther, faster.

- *People ask questions.* They challenge the status quo and look for a better way.

- *People create culture.* They interact with each other and form the backbone of an organization.

Thump-thump. Thump-thump.

Nothing gets done without people. In fact, I'll take it a step further and make this claim: *Any complex problem can be solved through people.*

As a result, leaders who want to achieve stellar results must start by focusing on the heartbeat of business—people. Heartbeat Leaders are uniquely prepared to dominate their industry because when you take care of people, you take care of the heart of an organization. Take care of the heart of the organization, and the entire enterprise will thrive. When it stops investing in people, any organization will keel over, hand to chest.

ORGANIZATIONAL CHEST PAINS

Unfortunately, what continues to drive organizations in corporate America is a focus on one thing. As long as executives get the results they want, they'll maintain the status quo, swapping out depleted people for fresh employees who don't yet show symptoms of heartbeat failure. It's only when the organization as a whole experiences pains that they discover there's a deeper heart problem keeping them from achieving truly phenomenal results.

Maybe you've felt some of these "chest pains" where you work:

- Your organization pays lip service to "people-first", but their actions tell a different story.

- All you see every day are people going through the motions, not living with passion, but doing the bare minimum just to meet the minimum requirements.

- You feel like you need 27 hours a day and 8 days a week to accomplish all that's expected of you.

- You're trying to balance your career and family, but your boss keeps setting unrealistic expectations and expecting you to miraculously deliver.

- Stress and pressure seem to be the norm, not the exception to the rule.

- Leaders pressure to simply "do more with less."

- The high turnover rate signals a revolving door for top talent.

- The focus is more on strategies and less on execution.

- Survey scores reveal consistently low employee engagement

- Revenues and profits decline steadily over time.

- Share value dips and continues to slide.

I get it. Over the course of my 25 years of leadership in some of the largest companies in corporate America, I discovered what it felt like to need more hours in the day to get it all done. I often felt overworked and underappreciated.

I led people who were frustrated because they were treated like one cog in the organizational machine, rather than as an individual with unique abilities to be maximized, refined, and invested in. I've felt overwhelmed by all the competing demands on my time and energy.

I've carried the frustration of knowing I needed to be great at work, but also keep enough in the tank for when I got home and exchanged my leader hat for my mom and wife hats.

Think for a moment about your own career journey. What have you experienced and seen in your corporate culture? Maybe you've felt this heartbeat pain and need a jumpstart or a bypass to reconnect to what matters most. Maybe you're feeling the pressure of a career blockage that causes your head to pound and blood pressure to rise. Maybe you feel overwhelmed by all the competing demands on your time and energy and don't know where to start.

Or maybe you've recognized there's a problem, but you haven't been able to put a name to it. You can feel the *thump-thump, thump-thump* in your chest, but instead of a gentle beat, it's a terrifying thud.

You may feel like you are the only one dealing with these issues. Trust me—you are not! This problem is bigger than you, but it's *not* stronger than you. Most importantly: there is hope for you to experience breakthrough career success by reconnecting to the heartbeat of leadership in a radical way.

A RADICAL RETHINKING

A true people-first approach requires a radical redefinition of leadership. I call it *Heartbeat Leadership*. It is a mindset that believes people are your greatest asset, your competitive advantage, and your key to solving complex business problems.

In heartbeat leadership, the leader's job is to empower, engage, and impact people, teams, and organizations to reach their highest potential. It's all about putting people first and trusting that the best results come from doing so. Some leaders act as if they've already done the work to get where they are—so now it's time to coast. *Uh-uh.* Not going to work. Your position of influence isn't where leadership ends—it's where you finally have an opportunity to do some good for—you guessed it—people.

> **THE TRUTH IS, THE HEART HEALTH OF YOUR ORGANIZATION BEGINS WITH YOU.**

The truth is, the heart health of your organization begins with you. Not your direct reports. Not your leader. Not that "other" department. It starts whenever *you* choose to take ownership of your own potential and influence.

Don't underestimate the power of your example. With your biological heart, your physical activity or inactivity affects your physical longevity. In the same way, your attention to your people impacts their longevity and success, which ultimately impacts your longevity and success. Investing in people is a win-win proposition.

Thump-thump. Thump-thump.

Every leader is a composite of the leaders who have influenced and inspired them. But sometimes you aren't close to those heroes—and you have to simply *be* the leader you want to see. That's what I had to do in my career because if I only imitated what I saw around me, I knew I wouldn't like myself. I knew I wouldn't position my team to thrive.

Some of my changes when rethinking leadership in the corporate world were instinctive, some were responses to what I saw while climbing the ladder, and some were inspired by how I would *have liked to be treated* when I was a younger employee.

I began making sure the heartbeat of my team was strong, by doing practical things like:

- Holding weekly or bi-weekly *one-on-ones with my direct reports and key cross-functional team members* to give people a chance to share regularly.

- Instituting formal interview feedback.

- Holding regular town halls and skip-level listening sessions

- Creating a program called JumpStart to get a new team acquainted with me

- Sending simple handwritten notes on birthdays and anniversaries

- Encouraging my team to be problem solvers

- Leveraging my drive time to do informal touchpoints with my team

- Making "people" an intentional agenda item in all meetings

These systems and habits weren't necessarily difficult to create, but their impact was extraordinary. Any one of them isn't the magical solution to all ills in business. But together, they reflect a way of thinking that, unfortunately, I have found to be radical when climbing the corporate ladder. A lot of leaders I interact with wanted to embrace a people-first approach in business, but they didn't know how without feeling like they were compromising results.

It doesn't have to be that way! I believe in *and* instead of *or.* You *can* be a people-first leader and achieve results. In fact, in my experience, being a people-first leader enabled my results and allowed me to work smarter, not harder.

I began to realize the health of my team was dependent upon me, their leader. When they were healthy emotionally and relationally, they produced and did their jobs well.

That doesn't mean you can fix everything. Just as in your personal health you can't change your genetics or internal biological hard-wiring, so leadership doesn't exist in a vacuum. You can't change everything about your organization or your industry. You can't change other people. Their personalities are mostly hardwired. Their work and life history have shaped who and what they are. But you *can* do your best to care for your team and invest in them.

On some occasions, I've been challenged that the people-first approach is too slow or too soft. Let's face it, understanding and interacting with people takes time. They're challenging and complicated. They aren't as easy to file away as a memo, email, or spreadsheet. They bring their problems and insecurities with them to work.

For all these reasons, some leaders want the quick solution: *Let's deal with the people stuff later.* But this short-sighted approach to leadership will hamstring you in the future—and cripple your leadership potential. Sometimes you have to slow down to speed up.

START AT THE BOTTOM. CLAW YOUR WAY UP.

When I graduated from college, I was a twenty-one-year-old, African-American female headed into a white, male-dominated industry. It wasn't a soft industry, nor was it a sexy one. As part of my first-year training, I worked as a sales rep. I drove an eighteen-foot-long truck, loaded products on a two-wheeler, checked-in products with store receivers, merchandised products, wrote orders, built displays, broke down and tied cardboard boxes from sunup to sundown. I hated every minute of it, but I knew it was a means to an end.

After a full year of doing this, I finally moved into my first leadership role and became the leader of men old enough to be my father or grandfather. You can imagine how well that went over. The corporate environment had chewed up and spit out older, more experienced, more powerful managers than me—but I was excited to serve.

Most of my peers, who were men, wore a button-down polo shirt, khaki pants, and functional shoes. It was far from what I considered to be my style. So I decided to *be* who I was instead of trying to fit in with the guys.

Each morning I moved the hanger with the polo aside and chose nice blouses, jewelry, and unique fashion statements. In fact, the one thing I was criticized most about was wearing high heels. It didn't take long to earn a nickname from my coworkers and my team—*Boss Lady*.

I put up with the condescending remarks and comments because guess what? *Boss Lady gets it done on her own terms.*

I chose not to work from sunup to sundown, even though the unwritten rule was to be the first one in and the last one out (or at least stay until the boss left). But at the end of my day, I'd done my job, and my team and customers were happy. People started to realize I was different. Being different is hard. It's doubly hard to succeed in someone else's world on your own terms.

I was determined to stay authentic to Dawn, the Boss Lady and leader I hoped to become. It took courage because it takes less grit to just do what is expected without upsetting the status quo.

But it was more important for me to be who I was made to be, so I could empower those who followed in my footsteps. Deep down I knew that I could have it all—the career, the family, the happiness that comes from knowing I am a leader worth following. So I persevered.

I had arrived with youthful enthusiasm and a lot of ideas but was often ignored or minimized. Some days I felt invisible and overlooked. As an African-American female in business, it would have been easy to become angry and disengaged, or worse, do only the bare minimum, or even leave the organization. (Maybe you feel that way right now. Know that this struggle isn't for nothing.)

My story, as painful as it was at times, laid the foundation for something new. Knowing the pain of invisibility, I never wanted anybody near me to feel that way. I vowed to redefine the culture of my team. Because I loved leading people and helping them become their best, I wanted to get as high in the organization as I possibly could to do the most good I could do.

If people weren't going to help me get there, then I would take the initiative to learn and grow on my own. Personal development became

I DECIDED OBSTACLES WOULD NOT STOP ME. THEY WOULD SHARPEN ME.

my passion. After investing in reading numerous leadership books, listening to countless tapes/CDs in the car, and attending seminars. I decided obstacles would not stop me. They would sharpen me.

My drive and determination were built on the following mission:

I will empower myself to become the leader I want to follow.

I will engage my team at every step of my journey.

I will impact my organization by developing teams,

delivering results, and challenging the status quo.

Eventually, my results began to speak for themselves. I remained focused on being the best version of myself. I made it a priority to control what I could control within the confines of my team and my areas of responsibility. I worked hard to build meaningful relationships that fostered communication between other departments.

It took grit and perseverance, but my drive to reach my goals exceeded the obstacles I faced. I wanted to prove to myself that I could do it. Most of all, my biggest motivation was to give hope to those coming behind me.

THE SIX PULSES

Along the way, I learned to be the kind of leader I wanted to follow and developed the lifeblood of *Heartbeat Leadership*. These six pulses of leadership informed all that I did individually and as a leader of large teams. They are the basis of what I teach when I coach leaders today.

Your heart is the life force within you. It's the organ that keeps you alive with every contraction and pulse. It constantly pushes and pulls blood through your arteries and veins to keep oxygen-rich blood flowing to and from your brain and other organs. In one sense, you don't have to do anything to keep your heart going. But your food choices, level of physical activity, and lifestyle choices can either help your heart do its job or cause it to malfunction.

Each pulse of your heart is either working efficiently and effectively or straining to keep you alive. As a leader, you are the life force of your team. Just as the heart pulses our nutrient-rich blood to each organ in the body, you push out encouragement, direction, correction, energy, growth, and influence to your team. And just like the automatic beat of your heart, you can make these pulses of leadership second-nature if you learn to recognize and continually choose them.

How you handle each pulse can empower or weaken your leadership, engage or disengage teams, or positively or negatively impact your organization.

We'll unpack each of these more in the pages that follow, but here is an overview of the Six Pulses of Leadership™:

Priorities: The Purpose of Leadership. Your priorities give you the gift of clarity and position your team to win. If priorities aren't crystal clear, you may find your ladder leaning against the wrong building and all you do will be in vain.

Preparation: The Energy of Leadership. Preparation is critical if you want to close the gap between where you are now and where you want or need to be. Only then can you start to move.

People: The Power of Leadership. People are your competitive advantage. Ensure you have the right people in the right seats, and commit to investing in them to achieve shared results.

Processes: The Drivers of Leadership. Processes are the drivers that simplify leadership. When put into place early, they enable you to measure success and mark consistent wins.

Performance: The Metrics of Leadership. Without measurable targets, it's impossible to know if you are succeeding. Performance metrics give you a system to measure, adjust, and repeat with laser-like focus.

Promotion: The Growth of Leadership. Promotion is the catalyst that helps your leadership grow. It is a delicate balance of humility and pride that shares your individual and your team's success with the organization.

At the end of the day, your team and co-workers want to know you're listening to them. It doesn't mean you do everything they ask you to do, but they need to know they have a seat at the table and that you value them.

They want to know that you recognize that they are the heart and soul of the organization. It won't always be easy—I promise you that, but cultivating these pulses, recognizing that people are the heartbeat of business, and finding ways to put them first will make you the kind of leader they will gladly follow into battle.

WHAT IS THE HEARTBEAT OF YOUR BUSINESS?

What if *you* dared to think differently about your problems and began to think people-first? How might that change your approach to leadership? Challenging the status quo always is a difficult process, but that's been one of the secrets to my success.

To think differently, I ...

- Initiated cross-functional collaboration vs. upholding functional silos and building walls...

- Prioritized my onboarding process and that of new hires, rather than leaving them to figure things out on their own...

- Committed to building teams of truth-tellers, rather than people who only told me what they thought I wanted to hear...

- Took responsibility for problems, rather than looking for places to assign blame or pass the buck...

- Integrated performance management, development plans, and feedback into the fabric of our work instead of letting them be only at certain times of the year.

As I look back over my twenty-five-plus-year career in corporate leadership and reflect on where I've been, I get excited for the future! Because there is nothing an organization can't achieve when its leaders learn that *people are the heartbeat of business!*

If you are someone who wants to empower yourself, engage your team, and impact your organization in a way that is congruent with who you are as a person, then keep reading.

When you learn to embrace the Six Pulses and put them to work in your own sphere of influence, the results will be nothing short of amazing. I've climbed the ladder through sixteen different roles and seen firsthand that it's true. That's why I *know* you can do it, too.

PULSE CHECK

Empower Yourself

 The truth is, the heart health of your organization begins with you. Not your direct reports. Not your leader. Not that "other" department. It starts whenever you choose to take ownership of your own potential and influence.

💓 Make sure you get to know your team members personally and professionally.

💓 Surround yourself with truth-tellers, rather than yes-people.

Engage Your Team

💓 Look for ways to collaborate across departments, striving to eliminate silos.

💓 An effective and considerate onboarding process is critical to a people-first approach.

Impact Your Organization

💓 Understand that people are just as essential to a thriving business as the heart is to a healthy body.

💓 Integrate performance management, development plans, and feedback into the fabric of employees' work instead of letting them be only at certain times of the year.

💓 It may be helpful to put out a survey to employees to measure their impression of how much the company puts people first. It is possible that *people-first* is just lip service and not actual practice, and a stakeholder survey would help flesh that out.

CHAPTER 2

PEOPLE &

What's the scariest thing that could happen to you as a leader? Getting fired? Getting sued? Losing money? What is it for you?

My biggest fear is becoming a leader I'm not proud of. Everything else I can recover from. But spending an entire career becoming a person you can't stand? That's a terrifying legacy.

I'd rather have a smaller office and paycheck *and* a career I'm proud of—for all the right reasons. Thankfully, *you can have all the above*, but pulling it all together requires a counterintuitive approach.

It's an approach I call *People &*.

Let me explain. Throughout my career, I've seen the trend of "recycling" people. If someone ran into trouble or was labeled a "performance problem," the leader would either yank that person out of the role or send them to another department for someone else to deal with, as opposed to simply letting them go. A 2019 poll of over 800 CEOs showed overwhelmingly the number-one concern they have is around attracting and retaining top talent[1], and according to the Work Institute's 2017 Retention Report, it costs employers 33% of a worker's annual salary to hire a replacement if that worker leaves. It's easy to see why doing some moving around instead of firing seems more fiscally responsible.

Now, I'm all for going green with my paper and plastic, but when it comes to people, dropping them into someone else's lap isn't solving the real problem. And it does nothing to help that person grow and perform better.

If there is a true performance issue, don't get me wrong: I'm not afraid to make the cut. If it's really not a good fit, both the company and the employee can get to healthier places in the long run if they cut ties. But recycling only moves the problem around.

I recall a situation where I had recently inherited a new team and was told that Roy was a very poor performer. After doing a little research, I discovered that Roy was a tenured employee and had been demoted a couple of times over the last few years. Instead of moving this employee to a new role, I took a moment. I knew there had to be two sides to the story. So, I called Roy into my office for a face-to-face conversation.

I could tell he was nervous when he stepped into my office, but I tried to put him at ease. "Hey Roy, let's talk. I understand you've been demoted a couple of times over the last couple of years. Can you talk to me a little about what's been going on? How would you assess your performance now and over the past couple of years? What feedback have you received?"

As he told me some interesting stories, the situation started to make sense. He was angry about the demotions and felt that no one explained why and never gave any real feedback. He also felt he had no one to advocate for him. As a result, he was disengaged and just going through the motions.

After hearing his story and heart for the company, I could see there were some performance issues, but nothing irreversible. It was true that his numbers and leadership weren't satisfactory, but I decided to take a chance on him.

"Roy, I'll be honest," I told him. "Your performance is not where it needs to be. But you're going to get a fair chance to improve—and you're not going to be alone." Then we walked through a performance improvement plan. It was tough for him to hear. But he communicated that in all his years at the company, he had never gotten this level of feedback—positive or negative. He was legitimately teary-eyed, but after years of feeling like a recycled has-been, he was finally, honestly seeing what could be.

In the end, the decision was in his hands. "If you want to improve and keep your job," I told him, "I'm here to support you. Or you can be bitter about it, not improve, and walk out the door now. You choose."

He asked to think about it for twenty-four hours. When he returned the next day, he was bright-eyed and eager to get to work. His entire demeanor had changed. "I believe you are genuine about supporting me," he reported. "I want my job and I'm willing to work to improve."

Roy diligently worked through the improvement plan. At the time of this writing, he still works there. But his performance reviews have radically changed for the better.

It would have been simpler to say, "Roy, you're not getting it done. It's time for you to go." But heartbeat leadership isn't about taking the easy road; it's about leading people well and helping them succeed. Every problem we face as leaders is ultimately a people problem in some way.

That's why we need to adopt a *People &* approach. In this case, the problem was Roy's poor performance results *and* a lack of genuine interaction with the actual person, Roy.

BUT RESULTS PAY THE BILLS

Roy's story is an encouraging one, but rare in the typical workplace climate. After all, which of the following statements do you think a leader would react to more positively? *I just increased profits by 5% and made us more money,* or, *I just had a difficult conversation with a new employee that put them on board with the company vision?*

If you're honest, which would *you* want to hear from your team member on the last Friday before the end of the fiscal quarter? Candidly, the corporate environment naturally expects, encourages, and rewards an emphasis on numbers, sometimes at the expense of developing people.

> **EVERY PROBLEM WE FACE AS LEADERS IS ULTIMATELY A PEOPLE PROBLEM IN SOME WAY.**

That's why the leaders focused solely on results might dismiss the people-first approach as being idealistic: This is the real world! *People &* sounds warm and fuzzy. The cold, hard bottom-line is what gets results, not relationships, right?

Well, you know what isn't warm and fuzzy? Turnover. Burnout. Disengagement. Sound familiar? Maybe you're one of those leaders who feels the pain: overworked with stress spilling into your family life. So you try harder and tell yourself, *Once I get through this next wave of projects I'll have time to do the things I love.*

But you're stuck on the hamster wheel. You're exhausted but can't afford to take a vacation because falling behind puts your *results-based* job at risk. Maybe that's why a staggering 212 million vacation days were unused in 2017.[2] Speaking of cold, hard numbers, that's an estimated $62.2 *billion* in lost benefits!

Working for the numbers is like sprinting in the 100m dash. There's a reason there isn't a "marathon sprint" in the Olympics. Pushing people so hard all the time only leads to high turnover rates instead of promotion and growth. As a result, leaders lose good people because the always-on-the-go culture suffocates them. People forget about a way up and start looking for a way out. Silos form between departments because everything becomes a competition, not a collaboration.

Results are a fickle currency. They're important, don't get me wrong, but working for results *alone* hurts more than just the company bottom line in the long run. It hurts your leadership effectiveness. According to an article entitled "8 Employee Engagement Statistics You Need to Know in 2020"[3], 85% of employees are not engaged in the workplace, and 81% of employees are considering leaving their job. This disengagement costs companies $450-$500 billion each year. Heartbeat leadership helps you engage your employees. Research shows that a highly- engaged workforce is 21% more profitable, and a healthy company culture increases revenue by a factor of 4!

I don't know about you, but in my experience, there were not many strategies that generated that type of return. *People &* is not only the right mindset to have, it's a profitable one.

ANY PROBLEM CAN BE FIXED THROUGH PEOPLE

How do you lead in a way that gets results *and* strengthens relationships with your people? It starts by changing the way you think about people. When confronted with a problem, most leaders try to solve it by tweaking production or adjusting a process. But every problem is ultimately connected to people. It's always a *People &* a waste problem or *People &* a revenue problem.

> RESEARCH SHOWS THAT A HIGHLY- ENGAGED WORKFORCE IS 21% MORE PROFITABLE, AND A HEALTHY COMPANY CULTURE INCREASES REVENUE BY A FACTOR OF 4!

That's the heart of the *People &* approach and why I believe every complex problem can be fixed through people. Think about it:

- Numbers are down? *You'll need people.*

- Morale is low? *Can't change it without people.*

- Culture is toxic? *Starts with people.*

- Need new tech solutions? *People provide innovation and know-how.*

- Production problem? *People will make that happen.*

An organization wouldn't exist without people to populate offices and connect with customers. But far too often, people are an afterthought. When leaders feel the pain of a problem, it can be easy to blame it on the people they lead. Nothing could be farther from the truth. More often than not, poor leadership is the problem, because poor leaders don't identify problems that plague their people and help create a plan to solve them.

When you embrace heartbeat leadership, your people's pain becomes your pain. Let's face it; no one likes pain. But it's your body's quickest way to tell you *something is wrong.* Any doctor knows treating symptoms without further investigation isn't in the patient's best interest. Someone could take an

> **WHEN LEADERS FEEL THE PAIN OF A PROBLEM, IT CAN BE EASY TO BLAME IT ON THE PEOPLE THEY LEAD. NOTHING COULD BE FARTHER FROM THE TRUTH.**

aspirin for a fever or an antacid for indigestion, but if the real problem is a case of the flu, no one will feel better until the deeper problem is addressed.

What's even more hazardous than an obviously ill person? Someone who no longer feels the pain. There's a rare but life-threatening condition called Congenital Insensitivity to Pain and Anhidrosis (CIPA) where the body literally *can't feel pain.* Sound too good to be true? It is. Parents of CIPA children struggle to detect the condition right away because for all appearances, their kids don't cry or complain as much as other children. But they're not avoiding injury; they just don't mention it because they're numb to it.

Without warning signals to the brain, CIPA individuals will walk over sharp objects, touch hot surfaces, or allow wounds to get dangerously infected—it's bad stuff—all because they don't feel the pain that warns of deeper dangers.

Far too many leaders suffer from a similar insensitivity to the pain their people experience every day. They see only results and consider people expendable commodities to achieve their goals. But symptoms of deeper danger, danger that will ultimately affect bottom-line results, always surface before the final numbers report.

If leaders keep overworking an exhausted workforce, dismissing employees at the first sign of struggle, silencing criticism, ignoring the opinions of others, they might as well schedule a coronary or wait for "the big one." Even if leaders can finagle the numbers to keep the C-Suite happy for another quarter, disaster is just around the corner.

Yet most businesses treat their equipment like assets and their people as expendable. This kind of thinking makes no sense. It's a rare meeting where the CEO says, *The #1 investment on our P&L should be our people.* But why is that so rare? How are people different from any other valuable asset?

I've spent a lot of time in warehouses, so here's an example I've witnessed firsthand. When a company is considering investing in a forklift or some other piece of equipment, they ask, "What's the return on investment?" They know that spending thousands, or sometimes hundreds of thousands of dollars on equipment is poor stewardship if you are just going to use it up and throw it out when it breaks. That never happens. In order to protect the investment, the leaders will first complete a training program on how to care for it and then purchase a maintenance plan for the new machinery to ensure longevity and continued value. They wouldn't—or shouldn't— invest in a forklift without a long-term maintenance plan to support it.

If that forklift stopped running at optimum capacity, broke down half the time, or could only lift a load half as high as it should, someone would take fast action to restore its full capacity. No business treats their equipment as disposable. They may depreciate it over time on paper, but while it's in use, they make sure to keep it working properly and at maximum capacity.

But leaders rarely extend their people the same courtesy. I have seen—and continue to see every day—new employees being hired without a formal training/onboarding plan. How many businesses maximize people, their most valuable assets, by investing in them and their "maintenance plan?"

You may know the pain of this firsthand, just like Roy. When did your leader last spend any time helping you get better at doing your job? For most people, it happens once a year at performance review time, and even then it's a cursory, "here's what you've done wrong" list or no feedback at all.

You may push for training, support, or personal development, but eventually you get tired of begging. Your morale falls, and soon you're running on fumes. You're like a forklift with crooked tires and low fuel that's leaking hydraulic fluid.

Often the lack of a plan is a circle of blame. The leader doesn't have time to invest in their team (or so they think). The VP thinks "all that people stuff" is a function of HR. The employee, meanwhile, just wants to do the job well and is frustrated with no direction and little positive feedback. Every action or inaction has intended and unintended consequences.

When you don't view your people as an asset, you won't see a need to invest in them. Your team members learn that they aren't as important as the numbers, so they do just enough to meet those objectives. You can almost see the light dim in their eyes as they dutifully fall in line.

PEOPLE ARE YOUR COMPETITIVE ADVANTAGE

Contrast that dimming effect with the leader who takes ownership of a team and creates a plan for growth. Does it take time out of a busy schedule? Of course, but this leader recognizes that a little investment on the front end produces exponential rewards later.

This leader realizes the power of *People &* and knows…

People are innovators. Technology has begun to advance at an exponential rate, but technology doesn't innovate. Only people do that. A forklift will never invent a better forklift, but people can. When people feel valued, they start a chain reaction of fresh ideas and cutting-edge business practices which brings more to your bottom line. Nurturing the bright minds of your team keeps the organization from the pain of stagnation and brings profitable ideas to the top.

> WHEN PEOPLE FEEL VALUED, THEY START A CHAIN REACTION OF FRESH IDEAS AND CUTTING-EDGE BUSINESS PRACTICES WHICH BRINGS MORE TO YOUR BOTTOM LINE.

People have heart. Computers don't empathize. Numbers don't roll with the punches and go above and beyond to create a WOW experience. You can't inspire an automated program. Customers like talking to people more than computers. No surprise there. People with heart create a company culture with heart—and that attracts top talent and grows the customer market.

People influence other people. Suppose I have two faulty forklifts. If I fix one of them and store it next to the other, the broken one won't change. But people can't help but influence each other. You can knock down an infinite number of dominoes by touching just one. Invest in one member of your team, and that person sets an example for others to follow and affects others.

People develop better processes. When people are allowed to learn, encouraged to experiment, and know they are supported, they will find the process that best benefits them and their organization. No one wants to do things the wrong way. Given the flexibility and authority to act, your people will find the best route from where you are to where you want to go.

People are more than the sum of their parts. When people come together, their combined strengths supplement and cancel out their individual weaknesses. No one person is the total package. How boring would that be? Some people are more vocal, others more reserved; some love a spreadsheet and crunching numbers, others shine like the sun in front of customers. A diverse team is more than just a group of individuals working together—they become a force for change.

People create culture. Look around your office and think about the culture. Culture is a combination of what people say and what they do. Culture is sort of an unseen force behind results. Create a culture where people can thrive, and results won't be far behind. Allow your culture to become cutthroat, siloed, or toxic, and results will plummet. According to Inc. com, companies with a people-first culture experienced 26% fewer mistakes, 22% higher productivity, and 41% lower absenteeism.[4] This positive impact goes straight to the bottom line. As a *People &* leader, you set the tone for your culture.

THE ESSENCE OF PEOPLE &

If you had to define your role as a leader in one sentence, what would you say? If you are results-focused, you'll likely say your role is to increase numbers or market share. But the truth is you'll always be limited in what you can accomplish on your own. There simply aren't enough hours in the day to do it all yourself. Believe me, I've been there.

If your role as a leader revolves around position and title, then you'll likely emphasize the climb. You'll feel like your role is to get noticed so you can move up the corporate ladder and get what you deserve. I've been there, too. When the view from the top wasn't what I imagined it to be, I had to redefine my priorities.

I'll share more about that story later, but I soon realized the one thing that didn't change, no matter my role or my targets, was the people I could influence. I learned that I couldn't do everything on my own, no matter how hard I tried. I learned that striving simply to climb the corporate ladder was exhausting and ultimately unrewarding.

But when I invested in the people I led—well, *that* made me come alive. And the more I invested in my team, the better our results. The more I got noticed for the work we were doing. That's when I realized that as a leader I had one main job: to serve my team and to remove obstacles to help them get where they wanted to go.

> **IF YOU WANT TO BUILD A LEADERSHIP LEGACY YOU CAN BE PROUD OF, YOU'VE GOT TO LOOK OUT FOR OTHERS.**

When I started talking about *servant leadership* in corporate America, some people seemed to think I had three heads. But to the people on my team who knew that I would do anything in my power to help them thrive in their roles, the term was a perfect fit. It's impossible to be *People &* without serving others. And it's impossible to display Heartbeat Leadership if your heart doesn't beat for people. They are your competitive advantage. If you serve them well, they'll do anything for you.

As a leader, you have a choice to make. If you want to build a leadership legacy you can be proud of, you've got to look out for others. A servant leader is a facilitator, a traffic cop, a mediator, a guide, a coach, a confidant. As a leader, I never claimed to know at all, but that didn't affect my ability to lead, problem-solve, or encourage others to thrive in their positions.

If you are tracking with me and buying into what I'm saying, that's great. But there's one thing you've got to keep in mind: you can't draw water from an empty well. You may have a strong desire to serve your team, but if you aren't investing in yourself, you'll have nothing of value to give.

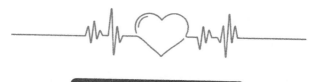

PULSE CHECK

Empower Yourself

💓 Leaders rarely leave legacies when they focus on numbers and the bottom line rather than their people.

💓 Heartbeat leadership isn't about taking the easy road; it's about leading people well and helping them succeed.

💓 When confronted with a problem, most leaders try to solve it by tweaking production or adjusting a process. But every problem is ultimately connected to people.

Engage Your Team

💓 When people come together, their combined strengths supplement and cancel out their individual weaknesses. No one person is the total package; lean into your team members' strengths.

Nurturing the bright minds of your team keeps the organization from the pain of stagnation and brings profitable ideas to the top. Invest in one member of your team, and that person sets an example for others to follow and affects others.

Impact Your Organization

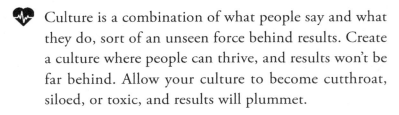 Many businesses treat their equipment as assets and their employees as expendable. It should be the other way around. When you don't view your people as an asset, you won't see a need to invest in them. Your team members learn that they aren't as important as the numbers, so they do just enough to meet those objectives.

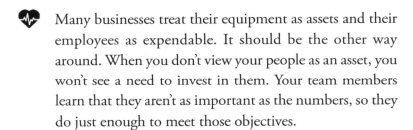 Culture is a combination of what people say and what they do, sort of an unseen force behind results. Create a culture where people can thrive, and results won't be far behind. Allow your culture to become cutthroat, siloed, or toxic, and results will plummet.

CHAPTER 3

IT STARTS WITH YOU

I was twelve years into my career, and I'd been striving toward my goal for over a decade when I was presented with an awesome opportunity to interview for a Director role. This was a newly-created spot and one of only four positions in the country. For me, it would represent the next level of executive leadership. Not only that, I would be the only African American female executive at this level in the field organization.

As you can imagine, I was super-excited about the opportunity, but I also had serious reservations from a personal perspective. I was a new mom and was navigating all that entails. My husband worked for Frito-Lay and was on the road three days a week. This position would require a relocation to the Detroit metropolitan area. I knew *no one* in the Detroit area, and if we moved, I would not have any family support.

Deep down in my heart of hearts, I knew that this was *not* the time to pursue this opportunity. Against my intuition, I pursued the opportunity anyway and interviewed for the role. Looking back, I realize I was more excited about the potential for opportunity than worried about the challenges I might face.

I figured this was my shot, and I'd better take advantage.

To make matters more challenging, after I interviewed for the role, I discovered from my boss that I would be appointed by a C-Suite Sponsor to the role. On the surface this sounds great, and it was very flattering, but it created a big problem. The local team—the people I'd be working with if I took the job—wanted someone else for the role. Because of this C-Suite leader's desire to have me in this role, they had no say in the decision. It was a recipe for friction right from the start.

I did some soul-searching, and after talking to my husband, I rationalized all the reasons why I should take the role. Finally, I accepted and got ready to move to Detroit.

When I arrived, I realized that not only had I ignored my intuition, but I had also severely underestimated what it would require to transition into this role. In my mind, I had been successful in all my previous roles, so I figured what worked before would work again.

Boy, was I wrong!

From the very first day, I knew that I had my work cut out for me. That first morning, I walked into a completely empty office. There was no welcoming committee. In fact, it was clear that I was *not wanted,* and no one made any effort to help me. Over the next few days, I discovered that the culture of this team was significantly different than anything I had ever experienced before. My leadership style that had been so successful before was clearly going to have to adapt; it would not work here.

It was a very challenging two-and-a-half years of my life, both professionally and personally. For the first time in my career, I didn't like my job. I didn't like the culture of the workplace. I was not getting the results I was used to, and I was angry with myself for not listening to my intuition.

I had two choices—I could blame the organization and be a victim, *or* I could take ownership of the situation and be victorious. I chose the latter. It was in my most difficult moment that I realized that I had lost sight of my core values, and that put me in a very difficult situation. As the old proverb states, *the only way out is through*, so I buckled down and set my heart on the best leadership I could provide. But from that day forward, I promised myself that my career decisions would be grounded in my life goals and values first. I was determined not to make the same mistake twice.

SUCCESS STARTS WITH YOU

Who is really holding *you* back? Is it "the Man"? The corporate machine? The Boss? The culture?

It's not easy to break through the glass ceiling. And that's true for anyone. Add gender expectations, workplace traditions, bias, stereotyping, and a culture of self-victimizing, and most people talk themselves out of even trying. As someone who has lived the journey, I can attest that it's not a walk in the park—especially if you approach with the wrong mindset.

When I entered the workforce, I saw all my problems through the only lens I could. Naturally, that lens was shaped by who I was as a young, African American female. I tended to think all my problems came from people who had a problem with that. But what I realized as I matured was that the feeling of being held back is something that happens to everybody.

I quickly realized that to take ownership of my career, I had to decide to become a certain kind of leader. I couldn't hope to defeat racism or eradicate sexism or have the path cleared of opponents or nay-sayers or toxic personalities without first changing the type of person I was as a leader. Unfortunately, those challenges come with the territory. You will encounter them and cannot always control them. But *who* you are is something you *can* control and use to your advantage.

YOU HAVE A CHOICE TO MAKE: BELIEVE SUCCESS IS POSSIBLE, OR COMPLAIN ABOUT ALL THE THINGS THAT ARE STACKED AGAINST YOU.

People spend months, years—decades even— complaining about everything that holds them back. Let me tell you, you can sink an entire career into excuses—and never see any change. No one else cares about your career like you do. No one else knows your goals. If you wait for someone else to invest the time, do the work, create the ideas, find the motivation, and wrap it up in a nice little package of inspiration—you will wait forever, probably still finding fault with everyone around you.

But, that's actually the best news—because that means you have ownership of the solution.

As one of only a handful of African American women in leadership in my company when I started the journey, I had few examples I could look up to. There were few mentors who could pass their wisdom on to me. So, my problem may have been different, but I discovered that the solution was the same—me.

To put it most simply: *success starts with you.*

I knew it would be an uphill climb, but I was committed to becoming a Heartbeat Leader, a servant leader who was the catalyst for my team's growth. I had no problem going first. I've been doing it my whole life. And I was willing to sacrifice if it meant I could help others achieve their goals.

You have a choice to make: believe success *is* possible, or complain about all the things that are stacked against you. I believe you have the ability. You have the resources. You have the heartbeat of the organization pumping all around you. It's up to you to tap in and take ownership. You'll soon see pieces of the glass ceiling falling around you and realize that when you take ownership, anything is possible.

DANGERS OF NOT TAKING OWNERSHIP

Leading can be a lonely business. Between the never-ending list of demands on your time and energy, a heartbeat leader often shoulders the burden of caring for the team. You want to invest in your people. You've got to keep one eye on results, another eye on your career path, a third on what's happening around you. And if you have any time left, you can try to have a life outside of work.

As you read my call to *take ownership,* you may be sighing: *I get it Dawn, but you should see my to-do list. You have no idea!* Actually, I do. I've been there, too. It's tiring having to climb uphill all the time. It's hard to be the first person to reach a milestone or to stand out from the crowd. But if you don't do it, who will?

We often fail to take ownership of our leadership for the same reasons we don't take control of our health. It takes work, planning, boldness and a willingness to swim against the current. And that is hard. Especially when you are fighting an internal battle you may not even be aware of, like these:

 A Victim's Mindset (*Everyone's against me because I'm ...*)

If you're the victim, you might as well give up now because you only have a couple of options. Do you plan on being saved? If not, do you plan to make a change? In the world of business, most people are too wrapped up in their own problems to spend their whole day sabotaging yours. This mindset actually blinds you to the real problems that might be happening on your team and among your people.

♥ Entitlement Thinking (*I thought I'd be there by now.*)

Really? The workforce is full of super-smart people. They all just want to get there. But you'll never get the reward without the work. If you think you "ought" to be somewhere, but aren't, ask yourself—what are the steps others have taken to get where I want to be? If you haven't taken those steps, don't be surprised that you aren't "there" yet.

♥ Lack of Self-Awareness (*I never really thought about that.*)

Like all of us, most people I coach have strengths they aren't even aware of. Plus, they don't understand their struggles. They don't have clarity on where they want to go, but they're shocked that they haven't gotten there yet. Let me challenge you to get to know yourself and what you're passionate about, then grow forward faster.

Long before most people actually raise a complaint or concern, the negative emotions have been swirling in the echo-chamber of their own heads. Some people live as if everyone else should know how they are feeling, a classic example of an unaware employee.

If you want to see change, you have to go first. Leadership attitudes are highly contagious. For better or for worse, *people do what people see.* If they see you do nothing, they do nothing. Even more damaging, when they see you do the wrong thing, or react out of your own insecurities and pain, they copy your example. So when you don't take ownership of your life, leadership, and career it does more than just affect you. It affects everyone around you as well.

Maybe you are unintentionally modeling some of these side effects of passive leadership, like shutting down communication. That's not ownership; that's avoidance. Or perhaps you start hoarding ideas. Cross-currents between team members and departments shut down because sharing a new, creative idea carries too much stress or risk. Ideas and creativity become a kind of currency that is traded and manipulated across teams.

> IF YOU WANT TO SEE CHANGE, YOU HAVE TO GO FIRST. LEADERSHIP ATTITUDES ARE HIGHLY CONTAGIOUS.

Perhaps if you are honest with yourself, you can identify other bad precedents negatively impacting your leadership and your team. John C. Maxwell says that everything rises and falls on leadership. I would go a step further and say that everything rises and falls on your own leadership.

It's time to be honest. Is your leadership inspiring or exasperating? Have you been blaming others for your lack of upward mobility? Have you done everything *in your power* to break through your glass ceiling?

If not, then it's time to make a change.

WORK LIKE YOUR LIFE DEPENDS ON IT

When I was fourteen years old, I got my first job. Like most kids, I realized the things I wanted cost money, so I started looking for a job. Growing up in Iowa, you didn't have to look very far to find corn. It was no surprise when I found a farmer looking for kids to help detassel corn. What *was* surprising was the $7.25 per hour that he promised to pay. I was intrigued, so I signed up.

The first morning was a shock. My dad dropped me off at a park bench at 3 o'clock in the morning. Over the next fifteen minutes, other sleepy kids stumbled to the curb, and we all loaded on a school bus to head to the cornfields. It took about an hour to get there, and by then we were more than ready to get off the bus.

If you've never heard of detasseling corn, here's a crash course. First, these corn fields weren't full of the cute corn-on-the-cob kind of corn. This was feeder corn. These corn stalks grew taller, had thicker leaves, and were primarily grown for animal consumption.

Stepping off that bus, it seemed like the rows of corn went on for days. Every other corn stalk was tagged with a red tag, and those red tags differentiated the male corn from the female corn.

The idea behind detasseling is to pull the tassel out of the top of the female corn, so the male corn can fertilize it. These rows can be a half-mile to a mile long *in one direction*. To earn my $7.25 per hour, I had to stand on my feet all day long with my arms raised above my head and pop the tassels out of the corn. My arms stayed in continual motion, pulling a tassel, dropping it to the ground, sliding down to the next red tag, and repeating the process. It was grueling manual labor.

Every day, I stood in the hot summer sun. But at five o'clock in the morning, the corn was wet, so they gave us garbage bags to use as ponchos. When the sun started to peek over the horizon, I shucked out of my poncho before it turned into a greenhouse. We were supposed to wear long sleeves because we'd get corn rash from the tassels brushing against bare skin. But it was so hot, I never did that. I worked in a tank top and wore my corn rash proudly.

If a thunderstorm popped up, we might beeline it back to the school bus for shelter. But other than that, it was sunup to sundown, ten to twelve hours a day, for a couple of weeks at a time.

Then at the end of every day we'd load on the bus—hot, sweaty, itchy, and sticky—for an hour-long ride back to the park. My parents would pick me up. I'd get home, grab something to eat, take a bath, go to bed, get back up, and do it again the next day.

Those crews lasted two weeks at a time. I didn't like the work, but I loved the money. I was motivated by the fact that I could earn good money and knew I could do anything for a short period of time.

I'm no stranger to hard work. In fact, a good work ethic was drilled into me as a child. I've had jobs ever since I can remember. Some paid; others didn't. In my family photo album are pictures of me at two years old, sitting on the bumper of the car, handing Dad tools while he was headfirst over the race car engine. I remember waking up before all the other kids on Saturday, carrying buckets and mops into apartments my dad rented out. While my friends were riding bikes, I was washing down walls and prepping for new tenants.

Developing my work ethic, grit, perseverance, and the ability to find solutions laid the groundwork that helped me get through the tough experiences I would face later in my career.

I'm thankful that my dad taught me the value of hard work. I didn't know it at the time, but my early jobs—detasseling corn, cleaning apartments, and even teaching violin—built a foundation for good future leadership. These experiences taught me what it meant to take charge of my potential and approach every job with an entrepreneurial mindset.

For me, the tipping point came when I changed my thinking from *entrepreneur* to *intrapreneur*. Then, my influence exploded when I taught the people on my team to embrace the *intrapreneur* mindset.

CRAFTING AN OWNERSHIP MINDSET

You're probably familiar with the term *entrepreneur*, but maybe you've never heard of an *intrapreneur*. An entrepreneur is someone who organizes or operates his or her own business and takes on the risk and responsibility of ensuring it succeeds. An intrapreneur is a person who applies those same principles of entrepreneurship to their role *within* a company.

> IF YOU WANT TO BECOME A HEARTBEAT LEADER WHO SHATTERS THE GLASS CEILING AND INSPIRES THE PEOPLE AROUND YOU, YOU'VE GOT TO LEARN TO THINK LIKE AN INTRAPRENEUR.

Intrapreneurs' names may not be on the sign, but they take ownership of their jobs by treating their area of responsibility as their business. As far as they're concerned, the buck stops with them.

When I think about all the jobs I've had, I've approached each of them with an intrapreneur mindset. I've shaped them to fit my skills and strengths. I didn't have to do it like everyone else. I put my own spin on my leadership and treated it like my own business.

I've always run my positions as my own business, even within the corporate framework. I guess I'm just not a "punch the clock, stay in the box, do things our way" kind of person. But that's because I knew my career was up to me. If I wanted to reach the level of success I aspired to, then I'd have to think differently and take charge.

If you want to become a heartbeat leader who shatters the glass ceiling and inspires the people around you, you've got to learn to think like an intrapreneur.

Intrapreneurs don't have to accept the status quo. If you've ever rented a house and dealt with absent landlords, you know the frustration of a poor status quo. There are only so many times the washing machine will leak all over your floor or the kitchen faucet sprays you in the face at 7:30 am, before you skip the middleman and just call the plumber yourself. (Or if you're like me, pick up the wrench yourself!)

Intrapreneurs take initiative. Spot a repetitive problem? Start solving it! You don't *have* to outsource your problems— neither do you have to solve it *all* yourself. There's a reason an organization needs a multi-level team. No one person can do it all. And when you wander into an area beyond your expertise, you can still solve problems if you are willing to join forces with those who know more.

Intrapreneurs change culture. It doesn't take much to get started. But your actions set the tone for how you want your business to be run—even if you're only in charge of a small team. Sometimes the simplest things have the most powerful impact. When I started to recognize people's birthdays and service anniversaries with hand-written cards, it seemed like no big deal to me, but the responses were amazing. I got thank-you notes back in response to my card. People wrote me things like, "I've worked at this company for twenty years, and I've never received a birthday card or recognition of my service." My administrative assistant had my deck of cards, and every month she brought me the birthdays and service anniversaries. When I was running the Chicago Market for Coca-Cola, 600 people received a holiday card from me in the mail. The reaction just from doing that alone blew my mind.

Intrapreneurs know a secret—treat your area of responsibility as *your business* and people throughout the organization will take notice.

OWN YOUR CAREER

When it comes to your career, you have a choice. You can either play the blame game and look for excuses that involve other people, or opt for the better way, which is to take ownership of your career and become the kind of leader others look up to. The truth is, the only thing holding you back is you. There are no problems so big that you can't find a way through them.

Be someone who doesn't blame others for your problems but finds solutions. Be the voice that inspires, not exasperates. Be the leader that others want to follow. Take ownership of your role, no matter where it is in the company. Become an intrapreneur who inspires others, and suddenly you'll see opportunities arise that weren't there before.

Best of all, you'll start to tear down the walls that divide people and build bridges that connect. Leadership rises and falls on *people*.

PULSE CHECK

Empower Yourself

An intrapreneur is a person who applies the principles of entrepreneurship to their role within a company. Intrapreneurs' names may not be on the sign, but they take ownership of their jobs by treating their area of responsibility as their business. As far as they're concerned, the buck stops with them.

If you think you "ought" to be somewhere, but aren't, ask yourself—what are the steps others have taken to get where you want to be? If you haven't taken those steps, don't be surprised that you aren't "there" yet.

We often fail to take ownership of our leadership for the same reasons we don't take control of our health. It takes work, planning, boldness and a willingness to swim against the current. And that is hard.

Engage Your Team

When you don't take ownership of your life, leadership, and career it does more than just affect you. It affects everyone around you as well.

There's a reason an organization needs a multi-level team. No one person can do it all. And when you wander into an area beyond your expertise, you can still solve problems if you are willing to join forces with those who know more.

Impact Your Organization

 Intrapreneurs know a secret—treat your area of responsibility as *your business* and people throughout the organization will take notice.

CHAPTER 4

GO WITH THE FLOW

know what you're thinking, and I don't blame you. You're trying to reconcile *People &* from Chapter 2 and *It Starts With You* from Chapter 3. Am I right?

It may seem like those two ideas cancel each other out. If you focus on people, then you take the focus off you. And if you take ownership of you, don't you have to become a little bit selfish to get what you want?

Not surprisingly, the answer to bridging both concepts is another foundational component of Heartbeat Leadership. It's not either/or, it's *both/and*. It's the head *and* the heart. It's the leader who goes first, *and* the encourager who pushes from behind. It's the sherpa who leads the team *and* realizes that each member plays a vital role in the climb.

How many times have you seen a heart just chilling on its own, *thump-thumping* down the street, out for a coffee, meeting up with friends, or making business calls? That would be weird, right? Disturbing, actually.

That's because the heart *never* works alone. At least not for long. It would be like a stand-up comedian telling jokes to an empty room. All the beating in the world is useless without a greater, connected purpose. The heart does amazing things as part of the circulatory system with arteries, veins, and vessels carrying blood to other organs in the body. There's a good reason that when your heart stops, you stop. It's that critical to the entire body.

Your circulatory system ensures that oxygenated blood gets distributed to all organs in the body. The stomach may be beneath the heart, but it sure isn't less important to living. No stomach? No food, no nutrients—no more living. The liver, the brain, muscles, skin, and every cell in the body thrive when the blood is pumping everywhere. Each part of the body plays an important role. Their differences make them uniquely important for the body's success. Their connectedness makes it all happen. Like a heart out on a stroll on its own, even brilliant leaders will be ineffective without a team.

In the last chapter, I showed you why it's important to take ownership of your career to become the kind of leader you can be proud of. People are selfish by default; no one needs to be taught to put their needs first. It starts when you are a toddler and everything you see is *Mine!*

If you've been a part of an organization for any length of time, you've probably bumped into people who still think like a toddler. They stick their nose into every project whether it's a good fit or not. They put their needs above those of their team. They look out for *numero uno* and move forward no matter who is in the way.

That isn't Heartbeat Leadership. In fact, it's not leadership at all. It's a mercenary bent on his or her own version of success. This type of person is so blinded by their own abilities that they are oblivious to the wealth of diversity around them.

They overlook people who look different, act different, and have different experiences and viewpoints. These people are so inwardly focused, they can't see anything but their own ambition.

Ironically, this myopic approach makes everyone have to work even harder. It's like a toolbox that's missing half the available tools. Sure, you can use a wrench to drive a nail, but it's going to take twice as long and be half as effective.

The parallels are obvious. Your people have their individual responsibilities within the team. The backgrounds, personality, and unique perspectives of a diverse team are all opportunities—and in both the short and long run. The leader who values this diversity and maximizes it can set his or her team apart.

Tapping into these new perspectives—really valuing each member as a complex and crucial piece—requires a free-flow of your heartbeat. I'm talking about inclusion and diversity.

> IF YOU THINK DIVERSITY IS JUST AN ATTEMPT TO BE POLITICALLY CORRECT, OR THAT IT TAKES TOO MUCH TIME OR ENERGY TO WORRY ABOUT, YOU MAY NEED TO REEVALUATE YOUR LEADERSHIP.

These two ideas have been hot-button issues lately and can scare some higher-ups away. *We don't indulge controversy.* Well, this one's not exactly what you might think. And you actually can't afford *not* to "indulge" in the circulatory heart-health of your teams. The legacy of your leadership, and the life of your company depends on it.

If you think diversity is just an attempt to be politically correct, or that it takes too much time or energy to worry about, you may need to reevaluate your leadership. The best leaders ensure diverse mixes of leaders, teams, and individuals work together as part of the bigger system. They understand the first step to ensuring organizational heart health is building in inclusivity at every step of the leader's journey.

THE MYTH OF THE SELF-MADE LEADER

Think about how you first came into your leadership role. Chances are it was by being the best at your position. I see it a lot in all organizations. Joe is the best salesperson in the department. We need a new sales team leader. Hey! Let's promote Joe. Maybe some of what made Joe such a great salesperson will rub off on the rest of the team.

But there's a big difference between being good at something on your own and being able to teach it to others. So when Joe moves up, he quickly gets frustrated. Things are different here. His team doesn't have his same mix of skills, background, experience, or drive. Are there some poor performers? Of course. But that's not the biggest problem. The biggest problem is this: Joe doesn't know how to harness the diversity in his team and put it to work.

So he defaults back to what worked in the past. He worked hard to be the best. He shoulders the load and presses forward. He believes the myth that if I stay self-focused, do it my way, I'll get better results. And for a while it works. Sure, he's burning the candle at both ends. But he's used to being on top, so his drive propels him. Except now he's the sales team leader *and* he's still calling on his biggest accounts. He's topping the sales leader board and his team coasts on what it has been doing. They aren't growing, and Joe is starting to burn out.

Like a lot of leaders, Joe failed to face reality: If you embrace diversity, you'll be healthier. Many workplaces are incredibly unbalanced. They serve a diverse set of consumers, yet inside they are homogenous—promoting the same kinds of people, with the same ideas, and the same basic experiences. It's a vicious cycle of sameness. It's no wonder the heartbeat of most organizations needs a jolt from a pacemaker to stay pumping.

BIG D AND LITTLE D

So what is diversity, and what does that have to do with Joe's (or any other leader's) success? It starts with something I call *Big D* and *Little d*.

Little d is what most people think of when they hear the word *diversity*. It's a wide range of options. To use a Coca-Cola analogy, it's the Freestyle machine with a seemingly endless mix of flavors and tastes. It's a mix of males and females, black and white, old and young, people-oriented and process-oriented, and everything in between. It's looking around the room and seeing faces that don't look just like yours. It's scanning the company email list and catching names that don't sound like yours. It's variety, spice, and flavor.

But as I've grown as a leader, I've come to see diversity is much bigger than that. In terms of the value that diversity can bring to the workplace, you have to think about *Big D*—Diversity.

Big D encompasses background, education, experiences, and culture. It's the things that have shaped you as a person and as a leader. It's the places you've succeeded in life and the places you've struggled. It's the mountains and the valleys. It's a combination of the university and the school of hard knocks. It's the mistakes you've made, the lessons you've learned, the people you've helped, and the dreams you've dreamed. It's much bigger than the exterior things we focus on when we look at each other.

Big D is what makes an organization vibrant. And *Big D* is the cardio workout that keeps your leadership heart beating strongly and circulates the best ideas and ways to thrive.

Most leaders claim to value diversity on paper. But if they repeatedly ignore the ideas, personalities, and backgrounds different from their own, they're sending a very mixed message to their team. Teams take these subliminal messages to heart and adapt their work to fit.

> THE HEARTBEAT LEADER WHO RESPECTS DIVERSITY UNLOCKS THE POWER OF A TEAM AND LETS THEM KNOW IT'S PRECISELY BECAUSE OF THEIR DIFFERENCES THAT THEY ARE VALUED.

Everyone hits the wall where they won't introduce new ideas anymore because every other time they've tried, they've been shut down. People who feel unappreciated for who they are won't bring their whole self to work—and won't ever share those creative, out-of-the-box ideas that could solve a huge business problem or provide enlightening perspectives.

The Heartbeat Leader who respects diversity unlocks the power of a team and lets them know it's precisely because of their differences that they are valued. When people feel valued they are more likely to speak up. The leader with the empowered team expands his or her vision and opportunity. Instead of carrying the burden alone, the Heartbeat Leader has a team to share the load.

RESPECTING DIVERSITY REMOVES BARRIERS AND ENGAGES

One of the most dangerous effects of poor company circulation is relationship barriers. Like a blood clot in an artery, it's much easier to build one up than to clear it out. And each clot increases your chances of a dangerous heart attack. A heartbeat has a specific job—each pulse pushes the blood around the circulatory system in the body.

If people are the heartbeat, they have to be able to communicate freely. Shutting them down or allowing them only to communicate at certain levels puts a lid on honesty, authenticity, creativity, and mobility for the company as a whole. Diversity and inclusion requires respecting *People &* their voices, regardless of who they are or where they come from.

Early in my career, I was regularly the only female and the only African-American. Age became a factor, too. Who wanted to stand up for the young woman who didn't look like them or act like them? Who wanted to hear what I had to say? It felt like no one.

Because of that reality, a dangerous, two-way obstacle formed. Since my opinions didn't seem to be valued, and I wasn't included in any decisions, my bitterness grew. Feeling invisible drove a lot of my frustration, even anger, in those first years. *Wow, is this what corporate America is really like? I feel invisible! When I speak in the meeting, it's as if I didn't say anything. The next person says the same thing—and it's the best thing since sliced bread.*

It was tough to assimilate. I was fresh out of college and in the management training program, so I felt like a fish out of water. Since there weren't many other young women, let alone women of color, even my being *in* the management training program was questioned. I heard people say, "They must have brought you in for affirmative action."

When you feel like everybody wants to see you sink or swim, it's difficult to build relationships. I remember distinctly always wanting to talk about who I was to coworkers and leaders around me. I wanted to show them the complex, well-rounded person I was becoming. I wanted to share my life outside of work, but my leader did not want me to engage in that conversation. It just wasn't fun to work for a person like that. Separating life and work so sharply didn't make sense to me. People don't actually do that—even if they pretend to.

Forget about skin color, or age, or gender for a moment. Wouldn't it be boring if everyone in the world *thought* the same way? There would be no interesting conversations because everyone would agree with what one person said. Heartbeat Leaders know that Big D diversity makes things *interesting*. It brings diverse ideas and experiences into the mix. It allows people to connect in ways that they normally wouldn't. And sometimes, it's the catalyst needed to jumpstart innovation and growth.

When people don't feel valued for who they are, their engagement levels plummet. As I mentioned earlier, according to a 2020 Smarp blog, a whopping 85% of workers are not engaged.[5] That means they show up each morning, stumble through the motions and then punch out. The next day, they do it all again. Think about how much that costs your company in lost productivity!

Hard work is part of any job. But hard work without connection? It's not sustainable for long. Expecting high energy output from your people without valuing their input is the surest way to bleed your team dry.

WHY HEARTBEAT LEADERS NEED TO EMBRACE DIVERSITY

I had felt the pain—firsthand—that a lack of diversity brings. As a leader in the corporate setting for over twenty-five years, I made it my mission to unblock the clogged arteries and embrace the freedom that diversity brings. One of my core values became diversity and inclusion.

When I moved to Chicago to work for Coca-Cola Refreshments, I was stunned at the *lack* of diversity. Chicago is a very diverse city with very diverse consumers, but you wouldn't have known it by looking at the makeup of the leadership teams there. There was less than 10% — and I'm talking obvious *Little d* metrics—diversity in the whole Chicago market team. But when I left it was up to 58%, which included *Big D* elements as well.

I truly believe if we had more Heartbeat Leaders, then Chief Diversity Officers and D & I departments would not be needed. The stories I still hear today are the same or worse than they were twenty-five years ago when it comes to diversity and inclusion. In my opinion, the reason it hasn't changed is we are treating it as a program instead of a core value. At the end of the day, lack of D & I in our cultures is a leadership issue, plain and simple.

I was intentional about recruiting and building teams that were diverse and inclusive on all fronts. For example, in one of my own experiences as a leader, I partnered with my HR colleague to gather the facts. Then we put processes in place for checks and balances on hiring practices to ensure diverse candidate slates and interview panels. My HR colleague and I participated in interviews at every level to set expectations and train the team on how to properly interview and select talent. We ensured all new hires got proper training and gave exit interviews and internal interview feedback/development plans for those who weren't selected for the job.

It wasn't just good for business; it was also the right thing to do. Because of this passion, throughout my entire career I was very involved with shaping and executing D & I strategy through my work leading Diversity and Inclusion Councils and employee resource groups. I was determined to tap into the power of the diversity at hand and use it to influence the culture.

My goal was to help make the overall culture better. But it went deeper than that for me personally. I remembered the pain in my heart when I felt alone and had no one to look up to or lean on. There was no Heartbeat Leadership because there wasn't much of a pulse. So I made a commitment to go the extra mile with people who were new to the organization. I offered to coach them and show them what a Heartbeat Leader looks like. It didn't matter who they were, I had a huge sensitivity to anybody new coming in. I knew what it was like not to see a friendly face or have a hand extended when needed.

The lack of diversity cripples creativity, stifles success, wrecks relationships, and crumbles culture. If you want to become a Heartbeat Leader, and apply the Six Pulses of Heartbeat Leadership, you've got to make a choice. You either tear down walls and build a diverse team whose differences become their strength, or you try to go it alone.

The health of your organization, like the health of the entire body, depends on integration without exception. Good circulatory systems have arteries, veins, and vessels that work together. Good organizations have diverse mixes of leaders, teams, and individuals that work together. A powerful difference between diversity (on paper) and inclusion in action is advocacy. That is, someone higher on the food chain taking the initiative to speak up and create space for the less heard. For example, I'm convinced that I ended up at Coca-Cola in a VP role from outside the organization because a Senior Leader recognized the lack of diversity and intentionally set out to find a diverse slate of candidates.

WHERE WE ARE GOING

Without a strong pulse, a body is headed for life support. Without the Six Pulses of Leadership beating strongly, a leader faces the same fate. By now, you can see that Heartbeat Leadership is what drove me to become the kind of leader I'd be proud to follow. It took a lot of ups and downs, but I finished my time in corporate America with a clear understanding of what it meant to lead myself and others well.

I discovered the heartbeat of any business is its people, and that as a leader, I had a *responsibility* to invest in people. I quickly realized that people weren't my problem, they were *solutions* to any problem I faced. That's why the *People &* approach became a key tenet of my leadership style. I also realized that unless I invested in me and made my

> I QUICKLY REALIZED THAT PEOPLE WEREN'T MY PROBLEM, THEY WERE SOLUTIONS TO ANY PROBLEM I FACED.

career path my own, I was going to drift and be at the mercy of everyone else's version of my career track.

In the rest of the book, we'll unpack the Six Pulses of Leadership: Priorities, Preparation, People, Processes, Performance, and Promotion. Each pulse helps you build the capacity to invest in people while delivering results. The Six Pulses are critical to becoming a leader who not only values people but empowers them to be their best.

You must first apply each pulse to your life and leadership. Then, and only then, can you teach those you lead and ensure that they become Heartbeat Leaders who contribute to the health and well-being of the organization.

PULSE CHECK

Empower Yourself

♥ When you feel like your voice isn't being heard, or that everybody wants to see you sink or swim, it's difficult to build relationships. Persist in connecting with colleagues on a personal level as well as a professional level.

♥ Try to go the extra mile with people who are new to the organization. Offer to coach them and show them what a Heartbeat Leader looks like. Be a friendly face and extend a hand when needed.

♥ Unless you invest in yourself and make your career path your own, you are going to drift and be at the mercy of everyone else's version of your career track.

Engage Your Team

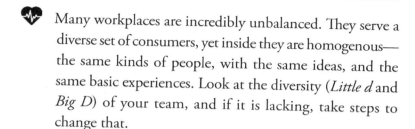

Many workplaces are incredibly unbalanced. They serve a diverse set of consumers, yet inside they are homogenous—the same kinds of people, with the same ideas, and the same basic experiences. Look at the diversity (*Little d* and *Big D*) of your team, and if it is lacking, take steps to change that.

Team members should feel they can communicate freely. Shutting them down or allowing them only to communicate at certain levels puts a lid on honesty, authenticity, creativity, and mobility for the team and company as a whole.

Impact Your Organization

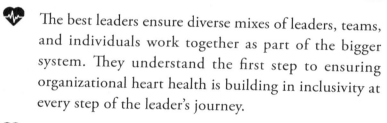

The best leaders ensure diverse mixes of leaders, teams, and individuals work together as part of the bigger system. They understand the first step to ensuring organizational heart health is building in inclusivity at every step of the leader's journey.

Before promoting from within, recognize that there is a big difference between being good at something as an individual and being able to teach it to others; just because an employee is the top salesperson doesn't mean he or she is automatically an excellent manager.

CHAPTER 5

PULSE 1: PRIORITIES

GIVE YOURSELF THE GIFT OF CLARITY

When you hear the word *priority,* what comes to mind? Is it the next item on your to-do list? Is it that emergency your boss just dumped on your desk? Or something that guides you and gives you clarity? Flip open your trusty dictionary—or tap open the app—and you'll see this definition: *something that you do or deal with first because it is more important or urgent than other things.*

How about when you pluralize the word and make it *priorities?* Businesses love to talk about their top priorities. But can you even have multiple priorities? How do you know which one thing to focus on or tackle first?

There's a good reason for Priorities to be at the starting line for the Six Pulses of Leadership™—if you aren't clear on your priorities, you'll bounce from fire to fire, getting sucked into the urgent, but not truly important, tasks. When that happens, you won't be able to lead yourself well. You won't be able to take charge of your career. And you can just forget about leading others well.

Understanding your priorities—personally and professionally—is that important.

> IF YOU AREN'T CLEAR ON YOUR PRIORITIES, YOU'LL BOUNCE FROM FIRE TO FIRE, GETTING SUCKED INTO THE URGENT, BUT NOT TRULY IMPORTANT, TASKS.

Priorities show you how getting clear on your personal and professional goals gives you the gift of clarity as a leader. And setting the right priorities for your team positions them to win. There is a thin line between acting and reacting, but defining your priorities helps you walk that line with the right focus.

What is the purpose of *your* leadership? It sounds like a simple question, but think about it before you answer. For some people, leadership is a title. A title is all about position. You are a leader because the sign on the door says so. This may provide recognition and power and authority, but does little to inspire people to follow you.

For others, leadership is a destination. They think that once they arrive, they'll earn the respect they crave. The problem with this attitude is—you never *really* arrive. Like a mirage, the finish line keeps moving, no matter how much progress you think you're making. If this is your version of leadership, the people you lead will see straight through to your motivations. They may follow orders because they have to, but they won't respect you.

Some see leadership as an opportunity. Leadership opens doors to impact others. It's an opportunity to share your skills with the people around you. To make them better. These people see leadership not as a way to be served, but rather as a way to serve others.

Others see leadership as a mission or calling. They know they have an ability to influence others to act, and they see it as a responsibility. Leading isn't optional; it's a mission. In their view, if you aren't leading, you aren't living.

Your journey to leadership only makes sense after you establish *clarity* around your destination. Leadership, like anything else in life, needs a purpose if it's going to make sense. Otherwise, it's just spinning your wheels. You can strive for your whole career and not make any progress. But that just leads to frustration and burnout.

Far too many people settle for busyness, not progress. They are moving, but towards what destination, and for what purpose?

The heart doesn't try to digest food; that's the job of the stomach. It doesn't try to stimulate the nervous system; that's the job of the brain. It doesn't process oxygen; that's the job of the lungs.

The heart does one job extremely well. It beats for its purpose. And its purpose is to beat. Every *thump-thump, thump-thump* moves the heart closer to its destination—pushing blood throughout the body so each of those other organs can do their jobs.

If the heart were a person, it could be frustrated about all the things that it's not. Or, it could recognize that by identifying its priority—being the pump that keeps the rest of the body alive—it fills a vital and important role that only it can do.

YOUR LEADERSHIP PURPOSE

Imagine climbing your whole life, finally getting to the top, and realizing—*oh, shoot, I climbed the wrong ladder!* You look out from the top, ready to be ecstatic, but instead, all you feel is let down. All the work you put in feels wasted, and you aren't sure where to go next.

It's what happens when you haven't clearly defined your priorities. You start climbing whatever ladder is nearby just because it's there. When you don't take ownership of your career and your leadership, any movement seems like good movement. And trust me, there will be plenty of people who think they know where you should go and how you should get there. They won't be shy about telling you—especially if you are a woman or a minority.

> **WHEN YOU DON'T TAKE OWNERSHIP OF YOUR CAREER AND YOUR LEADERSHIP, ANY MOVEMENT SEEMS LIKE GOOD MOVEMENT.**

Working hard is important, but if you get into an endless loop of working hard for things that don't really matter to you, you'll quickly become unhappy. I like to describe this as when the audio and video don't match. Internally, you believe one set of values is important. But externally, you aren't living them out. Your audio and video don't match.

There's another danger that can be just as frustrating: *wrongly* defined priorities. As Stephen R. Covey said, "If the ladder is not leaning against the right wall, every step we take just gets us to the wrong place faster."

When I took the job in Detroit, I was moving fast. My career track was on autopilot. A nudge here and a nudge there kept me on track. I was climbing the rungs of the corporate ladder with energy and enthusiasm. As I put my hands upon the final rung, the one that would put me face-to-face with what I *thought* I wanted, I encountered a drastically different view than what I had imagined. I hadn't listened to my gut; I had listened to my ambition—and paid the price. After all that hard work, my ladder was leaning against the wrong wall.

That season was one of the most difficult in my life. The ironic part is I was climbing the ladder of success in what I perceived to be the right way. Sure, I let some of my past frustrations guide my decision, but I had no doubt that I *could* do the job and make a difference.

It was a miserable two-and-a-half years, and it demolished my self-confidence. For the first time I wasn't getting the results I was used to getting. I faced the height of true blatant diversity and inclusion issues because they didn't want me there.

Without a corporate support system, I was running myself ragged on the job. I had little left in the tank when I got home, so it didn't take long for the mommy guilt to set in. When another job opened up, I jumped at the chance to move on, thinking it would make things better at home. But that job put me on the road two to three days out of the week.

It didn't help my guilt about not being the perfect wife and mom I wanted to be. I ended up in a place where I started having panic attacks every time I left the house. The bottom line was the guilt was so strong because I never wanted to have somebody else raising my kids.

When things start spiraling out of control, it doesn't take long to affect every part of your life. I didn't understand how things could have gotten so far off track. I'd always prided myself on being the lady with the plan. I was doing the right things but seemed to be moving farther and farther from where I wanted to be.

Have you felt that way? At some point in your career, you're probably going to find yourself in a place that you didn't want to be. You won't feel fulfilled, because the audio and video won't match. When you feel like this, life feels like an endless loop of frustration. No matter how fast you run, you're no closer to your goals. You're not happy with yourself. You're not happy with the people you work with.

You promised to pursue your goals, but seem to be working towards someone else's. The pulse of your priorities gets dangerously weak. Without some kind of intervention to spark new life into you, you're on a crash course with no way out. The flatline event is coming.

SOMETHING'S GOT TO CHANGE

It was about that time that I heard about a seminar called *The Corporate Athlete.* I signed up out of desperation, but what I learned there truly changed my life. During the seminar, I was forced to come face-to-face with my core values—those things I *said* were important. The speaker gave us an exercise that opened my eyes to what was missing.

He asked each person in the room to find a blank sheet of paper and a quiet place to work and start writing. He made me write down my life mission and my values. No excuses, no procrastinating. On the spot. I had never done this so directly before. Writing down what's important to *me* always seemed selfish. I knew I wanted to be a good wife and mom, a team player at work, and someone the organization could trust. Those were my priorities. But they were all outward focused.

I can vividly remember sitting at the table and starting to write. Once I started, it was like a river that had been dammed up finally burst through. I filled the entire paper with words. They gushed from my heart and soul in a flood of pain and frustration and excitement. Finally, I ran out of paper and I put my pen down. I took a deep, cleansing breath and embraced a turning point in my life.

The speaker walked back up to the front of the room and gave us one task. He spoke quietly and said, "Okay, so you wrote down what's important to you, now open up your calendar and tell me if you see those things listed anywhere." I didn't even need to look at my calendar to know. I'd been carrying the guilt of my mismatched values for over two years.

That day, I faced a tough epiphany. I had told anyone who would listen that my values were faith first, family second, and career third.

But the reality was my career was first, and it was killing me. It squeezed out everything else. I remember literally breaking down in that room. I knew I had to change something. I didn't want to be traveling three days a week. I wanted to be able to raise my kids myself. I wanted to enjoy my job, not be a slave to it. I knew that I couldn't continue to make life decisions based on my job. I had to decide what life I wanted and make my job *part* of that life, not *all* of it.

That day I vowed that I would no longer make decisions on the surface level. Things like job, money, and title dropped down my list of priorities. My job had to support what was important to me, not replace what was important to me.

Leaving that seminar I felt about a thousand pounds lighter. It was like I could breathe again. I didn't know the entire path forward, but I knew that by realigning my priorities, I'd given myself the gift of *clarity.* It was like scales

> MY JOB HAD TO SUPPORT WHAT WAS IMPORTANT TO ME, NOT REPLACE WHAT WAS IMPORTANT TO ME.

fell from my eyes, and I captured a glimpse of a brighter future.

I looked down at my list, and these eight values jumped off the page at me: *faith, family, friends, wellness, leadership, learning, diversity, and inclusion.* These values would form the basis of my decision-making compass going forward. I could see again, and the future looked bright.

YOUR DECISION-MAKING COMPASS

Not too many people these days pull out their trusty compass and use it to navigate direction. But paying attention to your heart and defining your priorities is a little more complicated than that. Knowing your priorities *and using them as the points on your decision-making compass* separates the leader who goes with the flow from the Heartbeat Leader who is going somewhere on purpose.

That activity, which forced me to get clear on my priorities, is why I'm an entrepreneur today. That moment is why I'm not still behind an executive desk at a job that could have supported me financially until I wanted to retire. I had a good position at Coca-Cola and would never have needed to move again, but I would've had to take on roles I wasn't passionate about. I would have started climbing another ladder that, although profitable, wasn't going to take me where I wanted to go.

> KNOWING YOUR PRIORITIES AND USING THEM AS THE POINTS ON YOUR DECISION-MAKING COMPASS SEPARATES THE LEADER WHO GOES WITH THE FLOW FROM THE HEARTBEAT LEADER WHO IS GOING SOMEWHERE ON PURPOSE.

By getting clarity on what I didn't want, as well as what I wanted, I created options for my future. It's one of my favorite things to teach my coaching clients because it causes them to have those *a-ha!* moments. They tell me *nobody* ever talked to them about making decisions based on core values. I've come to firmly believe that a healthy heart only comes when you make your career support the life you want. It's a total reversal of the norm.

There's an important reason Priorities is the first pulse of Heartbeat Leadership. Without priorities, you may as well be lost. You can't hope to lead others if you can't first lead yourself. Determining your priorities should be the *first* thing you do to make sure your ladder doesn't lean on the wrong wall.

To determine your priorities, you've got to start by answering these four questions:

 Who am I? It's very important to be self-aware. To get a clear understanding of your priorities, you must first discover who you are. The best way to do this is to examine your life so far. The highs and lows and successes and failures that make up your life often shape your priorities. Examine your history and think about what it tells you. As you learn what makes you tick, you'll see some things grow in importance and some things fade away.

 What do I stand for? Talk is cheap. Actions are expensive. To discover your priorities, you first need to know what you are really standing for. Try to take an objective view of how you see yourself. What do your actions say about you as a spouse, parent, friend, teammate, employee, boss, or leader?

For example, you may think you are standing for diversity, but have you surrounded yourself with people who look, think, act, and talk just like you? The point of this isn't to make you feel bad. Rather, it's to help you see how to align what you *say* you value with what you *show* you value.

 What do I want? It's safe to say that everyone wants to be valued, loved, respected, paid a good wage, and able to make a difference in the world. Everyone wants their life to count. But beyond these universal desires, there is a vast mix of desires that fuel people's motivations. They aren't necessarily wrong or right, but they are unique to you.

If you don't figure out what *you* want, you'll end up climbing someone else's ladder of success and being disappointed when you get to the top. Growth happens when you admit that you *can't have* it all. Insight happens when you admit that you *don't want* it all. In the space between those two, you can get real about what you'll pursue and what you'll give up.

> GROWTH HAPPENS WHEN YOU ADMIT THAT YOU CAN'T HAVE IT ALL. INSIGHT HAPPENS WHEN YOU ADMIT THAT YOU DON'T WANT IT ALL.

Every choice comes with a cost. Saying yes to one thing means saying no to another. Only you can make that decision and live with the consequences. Getting clear on *what* you want helps you create the life *that* you want.

Why do I want it? Knowing what you want is only half the battle. Knowing *why* you want it provides the motivation to fight. Think about this—few people love eating healthy, exercising all the time, and never eating sweets. But the desire to live a healthy life so you can be there for your kids and grandkids gives us the *motivation* to make the right choices.

Your *why* is unique to you. I knew I didn't want someone else raising my kids. That gave me the motivation to make a change and realign my values. Spend some time thinking about *why* you want what you want. It will quickly become apparent if your *why* is enough to push you forward. If the *why* isn't strong enough, it probably wasn't the right priority in the first place.

FEWER, BIGGER, BETTER

In business and in life, you won't have to wait long to find a fire that needs to be put out or a problem that needs solving. There's a strong push to chase after small priorities, fire drills, and crises—they provide quick wins, and quick wins can feel good. But it's a short term win that will always leave you wanting more.

People do what they like to do. And putting out fires makes you feel like a hero. Go in and save the day, and there's a big sense of accomplishment, but it never lasts. Another crisis is always just around the corner. It's always chaos when you operate that way. It's a rat race that *feels productive,* but it's never calm, and it rarely moves you toward your goals.

Some of the most important things you will create take *extended focus.* If you are continually being pulled away for the burst of endorphins and dopamine that comes from being the temporary hero, you won't get far on the things that matter.

What you reward is what you'll keep getting. This is as true personally as it is professionally. Leaders without a strong sense of priorities fall into the same traps over and over again. They don't reward the planning and are somehow surprised when the plan falls apart. They don't reward investing in people and then are surprised when morale drops and talented people take their talents elsewhere. They don't reward good systems and processes and are surprised when things break down and fall short of their quarterly numbers and goals. They don't recognize performance over time, but only recognize performance in the moment, and are surprised when it's a constant fire drill with little improvement.

Heartbeat leaders know a secret when it comes to priorities. Instead of more, more, more— they focus on *fewer, bigger, better.* What if you had fewer things to do, but those things were *the right things*? What if those things actually lined up with who you are? What if they matched up with what you stand for? What if they were things you actually *wanted* to do?

When you are clear on your priorities, you can make your problems line up for you. You can stop doing *more things* and start doing the *right things*. You can stop being busy and start being productive.

> HEARTBEAT LEADERS KNOW A SECRET WHEN IT COMES TO PRIORITIES. INSTEAD OF MORE, MORE, MORE—THEY FOCUS ON FEWER, BIGGER, BETTER.

Even better, as a Heartbeat Leader, you can teach your team how to set their priorities so they work in their areas of strength. They'll do things that feel natural to who they are. They'll know what the team and organization want and make sure to work in that direction.

A heartbeat that pumps consistently and deliberately is a powerful pulse that works behind the scenes to make everything better. You can't see it, but you can feel it working. A heart that is thudding out of control may have a powerful pulse, but it doesn't make things better. It makes things explode. It leads to stress, frustration, and ultimately illness that can affect the entire body.

As a leader, you determine the pulse of your priorities. Then you lead by example for your team. Give yourself the gift of clarity by defining your priorities, and you save yourself years of heartache and stress. And then, when you reach the top of your climb, the view will be incredible.

POSITION YOUR TEAM TO WIN

No one likes to be on a losing team. It zaps morale and kills momentum. Losing makes it hard to keep going day after day. Do you learn lessons by persevering in the face of adversity?

> HEARTBEAT LEADERS AREN'T JUST MOTIVATED BY THE WIN ITSELF; THEY ARE MOTIVATED BY THE CHALLENGE OF HELPING THEIR TEAM RISE TO GREATNESS.

Sure. But let's be real here—losing stinks. People like to win because winning is fun. It puts a smile on your face. It leads to recognition. It often leads to an increase in pay. It gets you noticed. Teams like to win for the same reasons. And leaders like to lead winning teams because it's rewarding, both personally and professionally. Heartbeat Leaders aren't just motivated by the win itself; they are motivated by the challenge of helping their team rise to greatness. They thrive on being the catalyst that ignites team performance.

But to lead a winning team, you need a clear goal. That's why it's so critical to have your personal and professional priorities defined and your ladder leaning against the right wall. The hard truth is this—if you aren't sure where you are going, how can you hope to lead your team there?

In business, what constitutes a win varies by team. In team sports, you know that the team with the highest number on the scoreboard wins. In business, defining a win often depends on how you define your priorities.

For one team, the priority may be to increase sales dollars. Another might want an increase in market share. A third might want to reduce accidents in the warehouse. Each of these might constitute a win for that *specific* team. But for another team, it's a loss or at least a net neutral.

Your team needs a scoreboard, and as their leader, you must define what it shows, how wins are calculated, and what you choose to reward. Setting your team up for a win requires preparation and consideration on your part, but once you've defined your team's priorities and communicated them effectively, you set everyone up for success.

CLEAR PRIORITIES MINIMIZE FRICTION

If I walked into your business and spent a week observing your team, what would I see? I could probably learn a lot by just watching them do their daily work. I'd discover how they interact with one another and if they had good camaraderie and chemistry. I'd be able to see if they worked well together toward a common goal or if they each seemed to be pushing in their own direction. Before long, I'd get a sense of whether they were working efficiently or just spinning their wheels.

Most importantly, I'd get to see whether coming to work for you each day was a success or a struggle.

Heartbeat leaders care about their team. They don't want to see them struggle. The *People &* approach requires that you empower your people to do their best. And the essence of taking ownership is that the responsibility to empower your team rests on your shoulders.

> **WITHOUT CLEAR PRIORITIES COMMUNICATED BY YOU, YOUR TEAM WILL STRUGGLE. THEY MAY NOT LOSE, BUT THEY WON'T WIN.**

The good news is they are looking for *your* leadership. They want *you* to take charge. And if you've done the hard work of giving yourself the gift of clarity, then your team will gladly follow where you want them to go.

Priorities that are clearly communicated, do several things:

 Clear priorities minimize confusion/ distractions. Just like you, your team won't have to look far to find a fire to put out. Business is complex, and keeping everything going in the right direction will naturally lead to problems needing a solution. But creating clarity around priorities minimizes distractions and keeps your team on the right track. It gives your team a filter to weed out the things that don't matter and focus on those that do.

 Clear priorities maximize workload/output. Think about when you know what you need to do *and* you have the time and space to do it. Are you productive? The answer is usually yes. Clear priorities have a way of maximizing your output.

By doing the right things more, you do more of the right things. The same principle applies to your team. Give them clarity around what to do and remove distractions so they can do it. The numbers will take care of themselves.

 Clear priorities optimize the workforce/team. When one person operates at high efficiency, they can get a lot done. But when a team operates at high efficiency, it's a multiple effect. Clarifying what's important empowers each member of the team to be their best, and that rubs off on the entire team. It's exponential effectiveness on a large scale.

Every leader understands the pain of trying to do too much. Heartbeat leaders understand that this problem is multiplied when priorities are unclear. The effort expended doesn't match up with the output delivered. Your team is counting on you to show them where to focus their attention and skills. The human brain can only do so many things. Giving your team too many goals to pursue hampers their ability to ever get any continuity. Provide them with a clear path forward, and they'll have the bandwidth to build the momentum that makes them a success.

CLEAR PRIORITIES GUIDE THE TEAM

The Pareto Principle states that twenty percent of your effort will produce eighty percent of your results. Yet many leaders get bogged down in things that don't matter. They spend time in the eighty percent and wonder why nothing changes. It's the tyranny of the urgent in action. If you don't define your team's priorities, someone else will. And what *they* decide is important will rarely position your team for a win.

> IF YOU DON'T DEFINE YOUR TEAM'S PRIORITIES, SOMEONE ELSE WILL. AND WHAT THEY DECIDE IS IMPORTANT WILL RARELY POSITION YOUR TEAM FOR A WIN.

Heartbeat leaders don't waste time on things that don't matter. But how do you discover what matters and what doesn't? You establish your *team* decision-making compass, much like you developed your *personal* decision-making compass.

 Who is on your team? Just as the heart plays a specific and unique role in your body, each member of your team plays a specific role on the team. It's unlikely that you have someone on your team who is good at *everything*. And even if you did, it's unfair to expect them to do it all. You must determine each team member's skills and ensure they are operating at peak performance. Heartbeat Leaders know *who* is on their team and they strive to position each person where they can thrive.

 What does your team stand for? Every team has an identity—whether they know it or not. Heartbeat Leaders help their team create an identity that they can rally around. Your team identity may be because of personality, results, passion, or something else. Knowing what your team stands for (great customer service, always closing the sale, being cross-functional leaders, etc.) gives them an identity they can be proud of.

What do you want to accomplish? Good teams create individual goals and team goals. Good leaders communicate those goals often. Creating clarity around your goals keeps things interesting and gives your team a better target to shoot for than just getting through the day and clocking out. It builds unity around common purpose and helps everyone rise to the occasion. The Heartbeat Leader leads the charge and rallies the team around the common mission.

 Why do you want to accomplish it? Connecting *what* you want to accomplish to *why* you want to accomplish it is the Heartbeat Leader's secret weapon. It circles back to who is on your team and what your team stands for. When people contribute from their area of strength and unite around a common mission, it taps something deep inside their souls; success becomes deeply rewarding.

As the leader, you are the priority gatekeeper. Your job is to protect and filter what flows down to your team in addition to advocating upstream. Too often I see leaders that just pass down direction from above with no thought to how the new direction impacts existing priorities, and it just becomes a pile on. When this happens, you force your team to make individual decisions on the priorities which may impede the collective success of the team.

> WHEN PEOPLE CONTRIBUTE FROM THEIR AREA OF STRENGTH AND UNITE AROUND A COMMON MISSION, IT TAPS SOMETHING DEEP INSIDE THEIR SOULS; SUCCESS BECOMES DEEPLY REWARDING.

By creating a team decision-making compass you ensure that your effort isn't wasted on the wrong things. Avoiding things that don't matter or don't yield the highest results equips you to focus on the right things. Your team decision-making compass becomes the lens through which you view everything else. That's the power of priorities. If you don't bring the core deliverables, none of the extra stuff matters.

HOW TO EMPOWER YOUR TEAM TO SUCCEED

Every business I've ever worked for or with is enamored by saying they have a strategy. But then they turn around and don't do anything with it. They spend weeks in meetings and create wonderful presentations. Then they present what they've created to the higher-ups. Everything looks good and shows how their strategy is going to deliver the numbers. And everyone is on board. The path is clear.

Then something strange happens. They abandon their hard-planned strategy and shoot from the hip. They do something completely different than their plan and wonder why it leads to frustration and chaos.

Heartbeat leaders think differently. They aren't rigidly tied to the plan, and they'll adapt where necessary, but they realize a clear plan provides clarity. They do what it takes to empower their team to succeed. If you want to set your team up to win, here are the steps:

1. **Define your priorities.** As the leader, you must develop the ability to turn high-level strategy into actionable priorities. You may be privy to information that your team is not aware of. You've got to decide what to share

and how this information fits in with your priorities. Once you've looked up at the big picture strategy and below to your team, you can define your priorities. Use your decision-making compass as a guide.

2. **Stick to your strategy.** It's easy to get distracted by the next big idea or a fire that consumes your energy. But if you want to position your team to win, you've got to stick to your strategy.

3. **Debate what's debatable.** To be fair, every strategy can use micro-adjustments. These tweaks keep the priorities in view but adjust the process along the way. Part of the way to do this is to debate what's debatable with your team. I'm the kind of person who will always push the boundaries.

    I had one boss who had an open-door policy and would encourage the team to bring ideas to him. So when I had an idea, I would list my pros and cons and let him know I thought through both sides. I'd show how I arrived at my decision and then pause to let him weigh in. Sometimes we'd debate and change the plan. Other times things would stay the same.

    As the leader, at the end of the day, you're the boss. If you say no, you say no. But you need to have a good reason. Sometimes things are flexible and can be changed. Other times, things are inflexible and your hands are tied. Let your team know which is which, and encourage them to be creative when it comes to pursuing priorities.

4. **Create a decision tree.** A decision tree enables your team to keep priorities top of mind and make easy decisions on which way to go. I always tried to give my team a decision tree. Does it tie to the strategy? Yes or no. If yes, then we should consider it. Does it contribute to the business plan? Yes or no. Decision trees make it easy to know whether or not to take action. They empower your team to take initiative and move toward the goal.

5. **Position your people to succeed.** Heartbeat leaders don't make assumptions about their teams; they *know* them and put them in the best place to succeed. Jim Collins calls it putting people in the right seat on the bus. Think about what needs you have to reach your goals. Then evaluate your team. Have you ensured that they are properly positioned to succeed? If not, shuffle the seats until the team members are in the right place.

6. **Lead the way.** Leaders lead. Heartbeat Leaders lead with courage and clarity. Knowing your priorities gives you confidence. Identifying the points on your decision-making compass—both personally and for your team—gives you the clarity you need to push forward. When you lead your team well, they will get behind you.

When you ensure that the leadership pulse of your priorities is beating with strength, it positions your team to win. And a team that wins is filled with people who are energized. They know they are valued by their leader (You!), and they feel equipped to do their job. The way forward is clear, and the leader leading the way is one they'll gladly follow. Positioning your team to win isn't optional; it's essential to Heartbeat Leadership.

PULSE CHECK

Empower Yourself

 If you aren't clear on your priorities, you'll bounce from fire to fire, getting sucked into the urgent, but not truly important, tasks. When that happens, you won't be able to lead yourself well. You won't be able to take charge of your career. And you can just forget about leading others well.

Priorities show you how getting clear on your personal and professional goals gives you the gift of clarity as a leader. And setting the right priorities for your team positions them to win.

By getting clarity on what you don't want, as well as what you do want, you create options for your future.

Engage Your Team

 As a Heartbeat Leader, you can teach your team how to set their priorities so they work in their areas of strength. They'll do things that feel natural to who they are. They'll know what the team and organization want and make sure to work in that direction.

Heartbeat Leaders aren't just motivated by the win itself; they are motivated by the challenge of helping their team rise to greatness. They thrive on being the catalyst that ignites team performance

Impact Your Organization

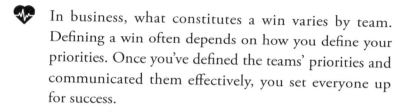 In business, what constitutes a win varies by team. Defining a win often depends on how you define your priorities. Once you've defined the teams' priorities and communicated them effectively, you set everyone up for success.

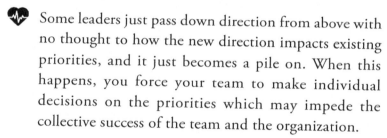 Some leaders just pass down direction from above with no thought to how the new direction impacts existing priorities, and it just becomes a pile on. When this happens, you force your team to make individual decisions on the priorities which may impede the collective success of the team and the organization.

CHAPTER 6

PULSE 2: PREPARATION

CLOSE THE GAP

Imagine walking onto a stage to deliver a monologue in front of a crowd of your peers. For some of you reading this right now, that's enough to cause you to break out in a cold sweat. According to the Chapman University 2019 Survey of American Fears, some 31% of Americans fear public speaking. In fact, it beat out the fear of snakes, abduction, and being mugged.[6]

But now imagine this monologue isn't just in front of a random crowd of your peers. You're in high school, and the people watching you are your friends. That ratchets up the pressure a notch or two.

You step up to the stage, confident you can deliver. You walk up to the mic, look out at the crowd, and get started. Things are going well until suddenly, they're not. Your throat is so dry it's like you swallowed a beach towel. Your palms, however, are so damp you know they must be dripping with sweat and creating puddles on the floor.

Your mind is blank because the thing you thought you were so prepared for is just—*gone!* You rack your brain for a word or phrase to get you back on track, but your brain has betrayed you. It's empty. The people in the audience wait patiently as you fidget and squirm to fight back panic.

It's no use. Whatever you thought you knew has left. Exit stage right.

Unfortunately, this isn't a fabricated story to make a point. This one is real, and it happened to me. In high school, I was no stranger to public speaking. I never set out to be a public speaker, but I ran for student government president and became used to being on stage.

This particular incident happened when I was giving a speech for the American Legion. They were having a contest on the Constitution, and every speaker had to memorize a part of it and deliver it from the stage.

Before that day, I'd worked hard for weeks to memorize my part. I was confident I knew it frontwards and backward. I'd practiced in front of a mirror so I'd look and sound "constitutional" I guess. I was excellent at memorizing things because as a musician, I would memorize my piece before a recital. It was important to me to be able to pull a piece from my memory and play it flawlessly.

That day, however, all my preparation was lost. When my mind went blank, I froze. It felt like I was glued to the stage. My feet were locked in place, and I couldn't move. I racked my brain for anything to help me, but I had nothing. My energy was zapped, and I finally had to turn and walk off the stage without finishing my recital from the Constitution.

The crowd was sympathetic. Everyone has been in a room where the performer messes up, and no one likes how that feels.

Some people call it secondhand embarrassment. Of course, I didn't win the prize. Even worse though, my confidence was shaken. I felt like I couldn't do anything that required memorization. I now needed notecards for speeches; I now needed my music for my recitals.

I had failed, but I wasn't done. I wasn't going to let this defeat me. Failure is feedback—it's not final. If anything, that lesson taught me to value preparation even more than I had before. I had tried something; it didn't work. Time to move forward.

When you fall short of your goal or underperform, you have to immediately begin thinking about what lessons you can learn and what feedback you receive. Most people don't do that. They feel sorry for themselves or just keep making the same mistake over and over again.

> **FAILURE IS FEEDBACK—IT'S NOT FINAL.**

But growth-minded individuals ask two questions: *What do I need to do differently next time?* and *What should I be doing instead?* They keep moving. It might be in a different direction. It might be the same direction again, but this time they're better prepared. Either way, when you get the opportunity to try again, you've got to be ready.

Winging it won't get you where you want to go.

BE READY

There are two types of people in the world, people who prepare and are as ready as possible for situations, contingencies, problems, and opportunities—and the people who wing it. To be sure, some of this difference has to do with how you are wired. If you are more methodical, it will affect your preparation skills. You'll likely have a system in place to help you prepare for anything and everything.

If you are this kind of person, you likely research everything. If you are flying into a new airport, you look up the map before your plane ever takes off. You've studied the terminal where you're going to land, identified the location of the restrooms and where you'd like to have lunch, and you know precisely how long it will take you to walk to the baggage claim and the car rental counter.

If you are spontaneous, you probably have a more laid-back approach to life. You like surprises. Not knowing what's behind door #2 can energize you. When you travel, you figure there will be a map in the concourse when you get off the plane. You'll follow the crowd to the restroom. The smell of something tasty will guide you to your lunch choice. This new airport is an adventure to be explored, and every new sight, sound, and smell is fuel for your mind.

So which is better? Neither *and* both.

It pays to be both spontaneous *and* methodical. Your brain needs surprises to keep you on your toes and make life interesting. But it also needs routine to keep you from being surprised in a way that is harmful or painful. Learning to balance the two and understand when to prepare and when to go with the flow is critical to a good life and good leadership.

The Heartbeat Leader understands the power of preparation and puts it to good use. That's why Preparation is the second of the Six Pulses of Leadership™. If you're serious about taking ownership of your career and serving the people you lead, then you need a plan. You can't just drift through your day and hope things turn out well. The organization you work for isn't a theme park there for your amusement. As the leader, you are expected to have the vision to see things from a long-term perspective and develop a plan to deal with them well before they become an issue.

There's a big difference between winging it and improvising. Winging it means you have little to no plan in place. You simply take the stage and hope for the best. You may do well a time or two, but you can't count on it consistently.

Improvisation is different. Heartbeat Leaders are great improvisers because they keep their fingers on the pulse of the organization, their counterparts, and the people they lead. They know how to act and react based on situations and circumstances. When you improvise, you have a plan, but it's a flexible plan. It's not chiseled in stone; it's written in pencil on a sheet of paper.

Winging it looks impressive when it works but foolhardy and unprepared when it doesn't. It doesn't inspire a lot of confidence in your leaders and can quickly go south.

Preparation separates the professional from the pretender. It shows that you take your job seriously and you want to be your best, so you can do your best. Being prepared doesn't mean you don't have fun. It means you know what you need to know so you can enjoy each step of the process. Preparation brings peace of mind. It also establishes you as a key asset that can be trusted to have a ready answer and a plan.

> PREPARATION SEPARATES THE PROFESSIONAL FROM THE PRETENDER. IT SHOWS THAT YOU TAKE YOUR JOB SERIOUSLY AND YOU WANT TO BE YOUR BEST, SO YOU CAN DO YOUR BEST.

When you prepare, you make the people around you better. You help them be their best because you've done the heavy lifting of thinking beforehand. You know each of their strengths and weaknesses and have a plan in place to maximize the former and minimize the latter.

People who are prepared almost seem to know the outcome before it ever happens. With preparation, action becomes automatic, friction is reduced, and the results speak for themselves. You don't have to wonder what will happen. You already know.

The heart doesn't have to decide if it's going to beat today, or how long each contraction will last, or if it's going to pump blood through every artery, vein, and capillary. It just does its job. The path is set; the action is electric, and blood flows everywhere it's supposed to. Heartbeat leaders operate in the same way. Preparation allows them to execute effectively on the work that they've already decided to do.

HOW TO PREPARE FOR ANYTHING AND EVERYTHING

Thomas Edison once said, "Unfortunately, there seems to be far more opportunity out there than ability...We should remember that good fortune often happens when opportunity meets with preparation."

When you are a young black woman in a male-dominated industry, and you are climbing the corporate ladder, you have to be ready for every opportunity that comes your way. You even have to be ready for the ones that you had no idea were coming your way.

It didn't take long for me to realize that the higher up you go, the less preparation time you're going to get, so you always need to *be ready*. The ironic thing is that if you spend enough time preparing, it looks like you are winging it because you are always ready. You've got something to say, so people don't realize you are actually prepared.

I used to be afraid of being caught off guard, so I developed some tips to be ready for anything and everything.

Always have something written down. When I was a young executive in a meeting, I noticed something about the people who seemed to be the most prepared—their pens were always moving and they were always writing something down. During the meeting, they'd have a legal pad open and were jotting notes as people were talking. I quickly realized that these notes did two things. First, they kept them engaged with the topic. We've all been in boring meetings before. Writing something, anything down keeps your mind in the mix. Second, writing things down gives them something to talk about. There's nothing worse than having your leader ask you about something *and you have nothing worthwhile to say.* It makes you look and feel like you don't belong. When you write down the things that are happening in a meeting, you will always have something to say.

Be ready to take your shot. Preparation can be a funny thing. You can do a lot of work ahead of time that never gets seen or used. The question then becomes, is that prep time wasted? I don't believe so. There have been a lot of times when I've overprepared. When it came to the meeting or the time to act, I didn't need half the things I had prepared for. But I'd rather be in that place all day long than need something and then not have it. You only get one shot to stand out. Leaders are always on stage, and you don't always get a chance to recover from a mistake. This is especially true when you're a minority female in nondominant situations. Preparedness in one situation can often be used elsewhere; it's not wasted. If nothing else, you can share it with somebody else to help set them up for success.

Know the questions before you're asked. Since that day when I forgot my speech in high school, I've spoken in front of thousands of people. As you can imagine, I'll always remember that situation, but it pushed me to grow and get better. Now, I'm confident on stage because I'm prepared. Even to this day, for every presentation I give—even ones I might have given before—I probably spend half an hour to one hour for every one to two minutes I'm speaking. I want to *over-deliver* value because I care about the people who are willing to sit and listen to what I have to say.

Realize there are no perfect plans. Even as a planner, I'm confident that there are no perfect plans. It's why Mike Tyson said, "Every fighter has a plan until they get punched in the mouth." Heartbeat leaders know that plans are important, but they also recognize that plans have to adapt enough to take a few punches and still survive.

> HEARTBEAT LEADERS KNOW THAT PLANS ARE IMPORTANT, BUT THEY ALSO RECOGNIZE THAT PLANS HAVE TO ADAPT ENOUGH TO TAKE A FEW PUNCHES AND STILL SURVIVE.

Leaders lead people, and people are unpredictable. If I'm on stage talking to a room of people, I never know how they are going to receive the message until I start talking. Then I have to read the room and adjust the plan. I can anticipate every question I think they'll have, but guess what? I'm a different person than the guy in the fourth row back, three seats in. His life experiences and worldview are different from mine.

If my plan is so rigid that I can't adapt to his question, then it's a bad plan. As a leader, you've got to use your insight, instincts, and intuition to prepare for the future. But then you actually have to push forward into the future and test it out. Preparation gives you confidence that you can move forward and adapt as needed. It closes the gap between fear and confidence and makes you a leader worth following.

START TO MOVE

You are electric. No seriously, I mean it.

Right now, as you sit in a chair and read this book, or scroll through it on your device, you are sending out electrical signals. Of course, you can't see them. No one around you can either, but that doesn't mean it's not happening.

Did you know that the most powerful source of electromagnetic energy in your body is your heart? It makes sense if you think about it. If you want to show off how toned your bicep is, your brain tells your arm to bend and contract the muscle. The same is true when you slam on the brakes in your car for a panic stop. Your brain tells your core to engage and you tighten up your abs to hold yourself upright, push your feet into the floor to keep from sliding forward, and tighten up your neck muscles to push your head back.

But try to energize your heart and make it beat. Go ahead, I'll wait.

You couldn't do it, right? That's because the heart is self-contained. That strong electromagnetic signal keeps it going until you die or you need a pacemaker to keep it going.

To get anything moving, you need energy. Energy is critical for movement. It's also critical for leadership. Have you ever worked for a low-energy leader? Their meetings are boring and disjointed. Their attention to detail is lacking. They do little to rally the troops, and consequently, morale is practically non-existent.

There are different ways energy manifests itself in people, but one thing is for sure: without energy, you'll have a hard time getting people to follow you. That's why the second pulse of Heartbeat Leadership—Preparation—is the actual energy of leadership. Preparation shows your team that you have a plan. It energizes them to do their thing because they know you've done your thing.

Energetic teams are prepared for action. They don't have to *think* about whether or not to act; they just act. When an opportunity arises, they boldly go forward, confident that prepared movement will lead to the desired outcome.

My son loves playing the Nintendo game, *MarioKart*. In the game, Mario and his friends race around different tracks battling each other for the lead. At the start of the game, every player is lined up at the starting line. As the light counts down from red to yellow to green, players get ready to hit the gas and take off. But there's a trick. If you hold down on the gas at just the right time, you'll take off with an extra boost of speed. But if you hold the gas down too early, your wheels will spin, and you'll lose valuable seconds as your competitors take off toward the goal.

To energize your team, you've got to have a goal in place, or you'll just take off spinning your wheels. A lot of leaders keep their teams busy but have very little to show for it. Prepping for the goal ensures that you are moving in the right direction at the right pace.

PREPARATION STARTS WITH A GOAL

Goals have always been important to me. Becoming a goal-setter started for me at the age of seven. I was always taught that when you start something you finish it—no matter what, whether you like it or not. If you committed to doing something, you had to see it through. If you got done with it, and you didn't want to do it again, great.

But you didn't quit. You pushed forward.

The mindset of *I am not a quitter* has always stuck with me and carried me along when things were tough. But if you keep getting yourself into situations you hate and want to quit, then you may be doing something wrong. It may be time to reevaluate the way you set goals and pursue objectives.

This is especially critical if you are a leader of a team. You can determine not to quit if it's just yourself you have to worry about. But when you've got a group of people who are looking at you for the energy to keep going, that can be draining. You may be able to carry the load for a while, but before long it will catch up to you and wear you down.

That's why it's critical to set the right goal *before* you start. This is true in your personal life, and it's true in your leadership. As a leader, the goal you set will determine the path your team takes. It may help to think of the goal as a finish line. When your team understands where the finish line is and you properly set them up to reach it, you've given them a good chance to succeed. Not all goals are worth pursuing. If you want to prepare your team for success, you've got to:

Set goals that align with your strategy. The first pulse of Heartbeat Leadership is Priorities. That's where you determine what exactly it is that you will focus on. Your priorities as a leader should align with your business plan. It's there that you take a high-level view of the organizational strategy. But I've discovered that most leaders use the word *strategy* pretty loosely. We abandon strategy in a heartbeat.

I get it. There are always going to be times when you've got to react. Work doesn't happen in a vacuum. Things in the marketplace change, people don't do what you expected them to do, and life throws you curveballs. It can be easy to get caught up in the here and now and abandon the strategy whenever something pressing comes along.

Good preparation eliminates the need for reactionary leadership. Sure there will be fires that you have to put out, but setting goals that align with your strategy ensures that you keep your eye on what's important. The pulse of Preparation empowers Heartbeat Leaders to take the long view.

When you set goals that align with strategy, it provides a roadmap you can use to then equip your team to do their jobs well. Preparation allows you to see the big picture and plan for the inevitable bumps along the way. You would never begin a road trip by jumping in the car, turning out of your driveway, hitting the nearest interstate, and just seeing how far you can make it until you run out of gas. You start with a destination, and you work backward from there. You know how far you can go on a tank of gas and plan to stop and fill up as needed. You determine how many miles you'd like to make it, but you remain flexible for the traffic jams, flat tires, and stops to admire the view.

Your team works the same way. You're driving the car; they're trusting you to be prepared to get them to the finish line safely. Strong leadership means you've got to be willing to push back when someone has an *urgent* issue. If it aligns with the goals you've set that push you closer to the finish line, then by all means, do what you have to do. But if the fire is because of someone's lack of preparation, then that's a different case. You've got to navigate that carefully.

Break your goals down into components and track them relentlessly. When I was a kid, one of my goals was to become an excellent roller skater. It's a strange feeling when you put those skates on for the first time. Not only are you about four inches taller (which changes your perception of the world around you), you're also much less stable than you were before.

Sounds a lot like leadership, doesn't it? You have to learn to see things from a new perspective and your feet don't feel secure under you. Without preparation, you can quickly find yourself on your backside with the world whizzing by around you.

When I was about seven years old, my dad would take my sister and me roller skating every Tuesday night. I didn't realize it at the time, but it was one of the first times I set a goal by breaking it down into measurable components. The first time we went skating, my dad held each of his little girls by the hand as we slipped, slid, scrambled, and scooched around the edge of the skating rink. His arms must have been worn out that night from holding each of us up.

A few weeks later, I was able to let go of Daddy's hand and venture a few feet away on my own power. I would fall a lot in the beginning because I really didn't know how to roller skate. But little by little, I was getting better.

What really helped me improve, though, was the way I tracked my goals. (I know what you're thinking, *what seven-year-old tracks their developing roller skating skills?* Above my bed, I put this cardboard poster where I had drawn out some lines with my Crayola magic markers. I put the Tuesday dates at the top and below each date, I'd write the number of times I fell. My goal was always to do one better the next week. So if I fell five times this Tuesday, I'd make it my goal to fall four or fewer times next week. Seeing my goal (zero falls) and my progress helped encourage me to get better.

As a leader, you can use the same process to encourage and empower your team. They can feel like they're on roller skates if they aren't prepared. Consider your strategy, outline the expectations you have for their progress and performance, and give them a way to track it. You don't have to look over their shoulder to keep them going. Tracking progress is often enough to encourage growth.

Be prepared to go a different way. There's one important thing to remember about planning. Things never work out according to plan. That's why you have to be flexible. If I wanted to leave my house in Atlanta and travel to Washington D.C., there are a number of ways I could get there. I could book a flight; that would be the quickest and most direct. I could drive my car on one of several routes that would take me north and east to D.C. That would give me the most control. I could hop on a bus or train. That would be the cheapest.

Which one should I take?

Of course, the answer depends on a number of factors that only I know the answer to. If I'm afraid to fly, then that's out, no matter how convenient it is. If my car isn't roadworthy, then I might have to rent a car or choose another option.

Being prepared often means you have to choose a new path along the way. One of my big goals at Frito-Lay. was to become a Zone Sales Leader. That was my destination. But there wasn't just a linear path that got me there. Having targets and something I was aspiring to kept me going, even when things got tough.

Even though it took me ten years to get there, everything that I did was always with that goal in mind. So when I changed positions, I would literally ask myself, *is this move going to help me reach my goal?* If I could answer yes, then I would make the move. Sometimes it seemed like a lateral move, but it eventually got me where I needed to go.

Preparation gives energy to action. It guides and directs you so that when the time comes to act, you aren't wasting time on *what* to do, you're busy doing it. Heartbeat Leaders are prepared. They know that their time—and that of their team—is valuable. It's a finite resource that, once lost, can never be recovered. Don't just spin your wheels, moving but making no progress. As you lead your team, be sure they understand the strategy. Create clear goals that they understand. Then follow up and over-communicate. Your people deserve nothing less.

PULSE CHECK

Empower Yourself

As the leader, you are expected to have the vision to see things from a long-term perspective and develop a plan to deal with them well before they become an issue.

When you prepare, you make the people around you better. You help them be their best because you've done the heavy lifting of thinking beforehand. You know each of their strengths and weaknesses and have a plan in place to maximize the former and minimize the latter.

Preparation gives you confidence that you can move forward and adapt as needed. It closes the gap between fear and confidence and makes you a leader worth following.

Engage Your Team

Energetic teams are prepared for action. They don't have to *think* about whether or not to act, they just act. When an opportunity arises, they boldly go forward, confident that prepared movement will lead to the desired outcome.

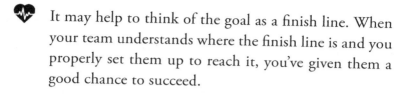 It may help to think of the goal as a finish line. When your team understands where the finish line is and you properly set them up to reach it, you've given them a good chance to succeed.

Consider the strategy you have for your team, outline the expectations you have for their progress and performance, and give them a way to track it. Tracking progress encourages growth.

Impact Your Organization

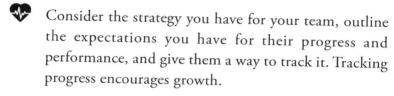 You can prepare your team to serve the organization well by being a talent pipeline, developing leaders who are ready to rise to any challenge and meet the organizational needs.

When your team helps solve complex problems through diligent preparation, you will impact the organization through your leadership.

CHAPTER 7

PULSE 3: PEOPLE

THE POWER OF LEADERSHIP

"Leadership is ultimately about influence and leverage. You are, after all, only one person. To be successful, you need to mobilize the energy of many others in your organization." [7]When I read these words in Michael D. Watkins' book, *The First 90 Days: Proven Strategies for Getting Up to Speed Faster and Smarter*, it was like fireworks shooting off inside my head.

Let me tell you something you probably already know: Leadership can, at times, be overwhelming. It can be a lonely job, especially if you are different from everyone else. But it doesn't have to be that way.

This is especially true if you move up into a role based on your performance. You may be great at that lower-level position, but need a whole different set of skills after a promotion. Many "leaders" get dumped into a new job without any idea of what is expected, how to succeed, or really even how to do the job well. Is it any wonder that people get frustrated and burned out?

Heartbeat leaders do things differently. They genuinely care for their people, so they do the hard work to help everyone succeed. They create options to win because they know that when their team wins, they win.

It always bothered me that there was so little consideration given to the onboarding process of new employees. If you think about how powerful people are, you quickly realize that preparing them to succeed helps you out in a number of unseen ways. When people are functioning at a high level (because of your leadership), they are more likely to see and solve problems, come up with innovative ideas, see opportunities that others miss, and a host of other benefits.

Onboarding has always been a big passion for me because it has been non-existent in many of my roles. Over twenty-six years, I held sixteen different roles. The first time I took on a new role, I surveyed my office and looked around for the *How to Do This Job* manual. It wasn't in any of the obvious places I was looking. Every job comes with an official job posting. That seems to be HR's best guess at what the job entails. It's usually a comprehensive list of everything that might possibly fall under your purview should you get the job.

But then there's the *actual* job. There's a vast difference between the two—a lesson I learned all too well when I moved to Michigan to take on a newly-formed Director position. I discovered from personal experience that people would benefit immensely from a 30-, 60-, or 90-day plan. They may be excited to tackle the challenge, but they often don't know what they don't know.

Enthusiasm is great, but it usually won't carry you through those first few months of getting to know your way around a new team, with new norms, values, traditions, expectations, leaders, and pressures.

Yet most people are just expected to figure it out. It's sink or swim.

In many organizations, it's like a badge of honor if you survive.

But Heartbeat Leaders think differently. Why make things harder for your people when you can make it *better* for your people? Why not shorten the learning curve and give them a fighting chance at success?

The third pulse of Heartbeat Leadership is *People*. Nothing works without them. Simply put, people are your competitive advantage. As Chris Fuller writes in *InSPIRED Leadership: Your Proven Path to Remarkable Results,* "You may not be responsible for the team you inherit, but you *are* responsible for the team you create."[8]

If you want to be a successful leader, you need to create a well-trained team that is ready to work. If people weren't delivering, I had no problem letting them go. But it's not right to show them the door when you've never properly trained them to do their job or set clear expectations for how they can succeed.

Good leaders tell people what they expect, teach them how to do it, show them how it's done, and then hold them accountable. There's a massive difference between deficiency of *skill* and deficiency of *will*.

Every time I had to make a tough decision about someone on my team, I always asked

> **THERE'S A MASSIVE DIFFERENCE BETWEEN DEFICIENCY OF SKILL AND DEFICIENCY OF WILL.**

the question, did we give that person the right tools to be successful? If the answer was yes, then absolutely—let's go through the performance management process. But if there was any question that we didn't do our part to help that individual be successful, then we owed them more. There may be a lot of warm bodies out there that can fill an empty position, but that doesn't mean they are ready to succeed. That is up to you.

EMPOWER YOUR PEOPLE TO WIN

I know what you're thinking: *Dawn, you have no idea how busy I am. Now I'm supposed to do HR's job for them?* I get it. I've been there. But what if by empowering your people to win, you win too? Wouldn't that be worth a little bit of extra work on the front end?

It sure was for me. Anytime I started a new position, I would remember this mantra: *Sometimes you've got to slow down to speed up.* If you are sitting in a traffic jam, you have two options. You can slow down and wait for traffic to clear. While you're sitting still you might pull up your GPS and hit the button that says search for alternate routes. You aren't moving yet, but perhaps there's a better route just ahead that gets you moving and avoids the logjam.

The second option is to speed up. Maybe you keep your left foot on the brake and impatiently rev the engine with your right foot. Then, once your engine is screaming, you let your foot off the brake pedal and rocket forward. There's only one problem with this plan—the car who's also stuck in traffic that's two feet in front of your bumper.

Sure, you may go really fast for two feet, but then *crunch*—your car collides with an immovable object and does hundreds or even thousands of dollars worth of damage.

That's how many leaders tackle a new leadership challenge. They are excited about their new job, and rightfully so. When I finally made it to Zone Sales Manager, I'd been dreaming for *ten years* about the opportunity. You think I didn't have big plans for Day 1? You bet I did.

But my team hadn't been waiting for me for ten years. In fact, we had just met. I had to slow down and get to know them before I could speed up and lay out my expectations. I had to ensure that they were trained to do the job well before I could ask them to do it.

Saying you don't have time to train your team or thinking it's someone else's job is cutting your nose off to spite your face. You're not setting your team up for success, and honestly, you're not leading well. You're certainly not leading with your heart.

You may not think you have time to train your people, but the truth is, you don't have time *not* to do it. Without clear direction, you're going to end up doing the same things again and again and again. It's the very definition of insanity.

Why not invest thirty days and get it done correctly? Better still, why not keep track of the process you use for onboarding that person so it can be replicated? The prototype is always the most difficult to create. After that, you simply refine it until it's perfect.

> SAYING YOU DON'T HAVE TIME TO TRAIN YOUR TEAM OR THINKING IT'S SOMEONE ELSE'S JOB IS CUTTING YOUR NOSE OFF TO SPITE YOUR FACE.

That's what I began to do with each new position. Since I didn't have the tools I needed, I went back to school, not literally but figuratively. I realized I had a problem. So I decided to find resources, study to find a solution, practice applying it, and show people how to do the job. I started my own sort of in-house, on-the-job training company.

Why? Because people are important to me, and I wanted them to win. I read *The First 90 Days* by Michael Watkins and *The New Leader's 100-Day Action Plan: How to Take Charge,*

Build Your Team, and Get Immediate Results by George Bradt. Before long, they were covered in scribbled notes, colored highlighter, and filled with dog-eared pages because they helped me get the job done.

Soon word started getting out. When people had a problem with people, they'd say, "Go talk to Dawn." Just like one heartbeat pushes blood throughout the entire body, my little heartbeat for people was beginning to reach different parts of the organization. I started sharing what I was doing out of my own need for survival, and it helped other people in other departments.

Even more than that, it solidified my desire to coach and train others. If you ever meet me in person, you'll know I am passionate about leadership and people development. I knew from firsthand experience how frustrating it was to have big plans for your leadership role and not know where to start. I figured if I could cut down on some of the learning time and frustration others were feeling, then that would be a good thing for everyone.

KNOW YOUR PEOPLE

When you look around at your team, what do you see? Perhaps a better question to ask is *who* do you see? Every team is made up of individuals who fill a role. Perhaps some focus on sales. Others focus on billing or accounting. Some may be customer service reps. Those labels may describe the jobs they do, but what do you know about who they are as people?

Every person who fills a role on your team has a life outside the office. They have relationships with others, hopes for the future, career aspirations, strengths, and struggles. It's more than just about what they can produce for you and what they are responsible for. Knowing your people is about who they are as individuals and human beings. When you know what's important to them in life in general you can tap into what motivates them. It's true that people don't care how much you know until they know how much you care.

Yet, a lot of leaders make this more complicated than it needs to be. If you asked me, *How do you get to know your people as a leader?* I'd start by saying to sit down and talk to them. That's how you get to know anybody, right? This works whether you are a new leader on a team or an existing leader who just isn't gelling with your team.

The reason things seem awkward may be because you really don't *know* your team. Again, this shouldn't be complicated. You work with these people each day; it is to everyone's benefit to get to know one another. The best way to get to know your team is to spend some one-on-one time with them. You can do this either in their environments or at lunch or over coffee. The idea is to break down the walls between "boss" and "employee." Keep it casual.

Start by asking them to tell you a little bit about themselves. Do they have a family? What are their hobbies? Where are they trying to go in their career? What are their goals and objectives? Use their answers to help you answer this question: How can I be supportive of each of them?

If you work in a primarily results-driven culture, quite frankly, this approach can seem like a waste of time. But you have to remember it's *People &*. You can get anything done as long as you value people. They are your competitive advantage and can push you to the top. Does this approach require an investment of your time? Of course, but it's an up-front time investment that pays dividends on the backend.

If you don't believe me, think about a leader who took the time to get to know you and helped you on your journey. What do you feel when you think of that leader? When people know you care and know you understand who they are as individuals, they will run through walls for you.

Here's the bottom line. At the end of the day, if something's not going well in someone's personal life, it's going to show up in the work environment. This happens whether you think it will or not. Life happens to everyone and, good or bad, it's going to impact a person's ability to perform in the workplace.

If people are upset about the work environment itself, it will impact work performance. If they are upset about what's going on at home, it will affect their work performance. The good news is I've found engagement can flip from negative to positive quickly if you are intentional about getting to *know* your people.

A lot of people think leaders have to have all the answers. It's quite the opposite actually. There's no better way to engage people than to ask people about *their* point of view. When you ask, "How do I help you do what you've been brought in to do?", it empowers the person. It shows them you respect them and want to understand how they work best so you can help them be their best. It doesn't mean you have to act on everything you hear, but when you connect enough points of view, you can discover the common theme among your people.

> LIFE HAPPENS TO EVERYONE AND, GOOD OR BAD, IT'S GOING TO IMPACT A PERSON'S ABILITY TO PERFORM IN THE WORKPLACE.

Another way to get to know your people is through a team exercise called a New Leader Assimilation. This is a process done about 60 to 90 days into a new role and facilitated by your HR team. The goal is to solicit feedback from the team on their first 90-day observations and what they would still like to know about you. It also gives you a chance to set expectations, share more about yourself, and deliver some quick wins.

DEVELOP YOUR PEOPLE

Think back for a moment to your own leadership journey. Did you go it alone, or were there people there to help you along the way? Whether you had great mentors or not, one thing is true—the distance between where you are and where you want to be is shortened when someone who knows the way invests in you.

Why should a leader take the time to develop their people? It's simple. A rising tide lifts all boats. It's never a waste of time to invest in your team. It's not selfish to want to help make your people better so you get better results.

> IT'S NEVER A WASTE OF TIME TO INVEST IN YOUR TEAM. IT'S NOT SELFISH TO WANT TO HELP MAKE YOUR PEOPLE BETTER SO YOU GET BETTER RESULTS.

If you've taken the time to get to know your people, then starting to develop them is an easy next step. Knowing them means you've seen them at work in their roles. You know their strengths and weaknesses. You see opportunities where they can thrive. Most of all, you know where they are trying to go next.

People with high potential want to do their job well for you, but they also want to grow within the company. The challenge for some is that they want to grow too far too fast. Of course, you're always going to have some people who say they are good just where they are. They may be close to retirement or just happy in their role. You'll also have younger people coming in and ready to become the next VP.

Understanding what their goals and objectives are, why they are working for the organization, what's in it for them, and what they want to get out of working for this organization has to be a two-way street. It begins by setting realistic expectations.

Once you know where people want to go, you can start to help them get there. I begin by asking a simple question: Why do you want *that* job? The answer helps determine if that's a good fit and if they've got the right experiences to get there. Remember, if you've taken the time to get to know your people, you'll have relational capital in the bank with them. You will have the authority and the trust to speak hard truths into their expectations.

One of the best ways to set realistic expectations is to pull the description of the job they want to pursue. Then together, in a one-on-one session, do an assessment of the goals, qualifications, and skillsets required to do that job. You can objectively help them see what they have and what they lack. It's a pretty eye-opening process for people sometimes because they just don't have that level of self-awareness. Sometimes people don't really know what those jobs entail. They understand the title or the intangibles of the job but don't understand the details.

Most job descriptions have the requirements, the specific skills, and the competencies that managers are looking for. It makes it easy to walk through the needs and assess whether they are present or not in the person. At the end of the exercise, I ask, *If the job were available today, would you be able to interview and successfully land that job?*

If you know the employee well, you can offer your point of view, too. You can also help them create a game plan to fill gaps and develop skills they need to be ready to move up.

The sad truth is that in most corporate settings, there are not a lot of development conversations. Many companies may say people are their greatest asset, but their actions tell a different story. In most of my career, development conversations didn't really happen unless I made them happen. Early in my career, I'd get some feedback at my year-end review or maybe twice a year. I knew this wasn't going to help me get where I needed to go, and it sent the message that I wasn't important. I vowed *not* to make my people feel this way when I became a leader.

Let me pause here and express what you may be thinking: *Dawn, if I help all my people grow and move on to different jobs, then I won't be left with anybody on my team. How do I ensure they do a good job while they are also growing forward?*

That's a great question.

In fact, on coaching calls, I have those conversations all the time. Part of the answer comes down to scope and scale. Many times, the job someone is doing for you will involve the same skill set they'll need for the next job. So if you help them improve that set of skills, you are not only preparing them for their next job, you're equipping them to be better at their current job.

The other key thing to remember is the *sphere of influence*. If leadership is influence, then it follows that by expanding your influence, you've expanded your leadership. As a Heartbeat Leader, you not only have to help people improve their skills, you also have to help them improve their influence.

Developing your people has to be intentional, but it should also be flexible enough to work with each person where they are. When you understand each person, you can implement a plan for growth.

RECOGNIZE YOUR PEOPLE

Do you remember in your high school yearbook when your peers voted people *Most Likely to Succeed,* or *Most Athletic,* or *Most Likely to be Elected President,* or some other superlative? If you're like me, you can probably see those pages in your mind right now. You may even be on one of those pages.

Sure those are fun, but why do it? The reason is simple. It's fun to recognize greatness (or at least *potential* greatness) in people. Most of those predictions won't come true, but it builds camaraderie and memories around shared experiences.

It's even more rewarding when, as a leader, you recognize the greatness in your people. When you know people and grow people, it's only natural to want to *show off* those people. When you work hard to help your people succeed in their jobs and move up in their career path, it reflects on you. You deserve to show them off.

Inspect what you expect. You've got to spend enough time with your team to recognize when they are performing well. You have to make sure expectations are clear and that you have a way to measure performance. When you recognize the right activities and behaviors that lead to great results, it's like magic. It's a simple thought, but what gets rewarded gets done. So when you see someone doing a great job, let them know. When they consistently do a great job, let everyone know. Try to catch people doing the *right* thing instead of focusing on people doing the *wrong* things, and you may be surprised at the results.

Give people the right tools. Most people want to do their job well. They want to be successful. They want to stand out for the right reasons. As a leader, it's up to you to give them the tools to do their job.

Stay humble. Some leaders let their power go to their heads. They forget what it's like to be in the trenches doing the work. Heartbeat leaders don't forget that the people they are leading are *people*. Just like you, they get stressed. Just like you, they have a life outside of work. Just like you, they have insecurities and fears—and you shouldn't be one of them. Set them up for success by leading well. It will benefit everyone in the long run.

Set clear expectations. What if I told you right now to put this book down and go drive. Where would you go? If you were hungry, perhaps to a restaurant. If you were out of milk, perhaps to the grocery store. If you were stubborn, perhaps nowhere! Without directions, why move at all? Many leaders don't set clear expectations, so their people are left to read between the lines and figure things out on their own. It's like taking off in a race with no idea where the finish line is. Sure, you can run hard, but you'll never know if you are heading in the right direction.

When it comes to expectations, you can never over-communicate. Tell your team what you expect. Write it down. Send it in an email. Put it on a whiteboard. Have the confidence to lead them to the summit, and explain how you expect them to help get you there. Clear expectations require courage from the leader, but they are invaluable to the people they lead.

Hold people accountable. In my opinion, accountability is severely lacking today. As a leader, it takes work to hold people accountable. You have to put time in to hold people accountable.

But many leaders won't do it because they don't want to step on anyone's toes. Or, they lord their leadership over their team, and they act in a manner of compliance rather than engagement.

Accountability asks the tough questions. Why didn't we get that done? What happened? What are you going to do about it? When are you going to do it? Then it circles back to expectations—if you don't do it, here are the consequences.

When you remember that your people are people, give them the right tools, set expectations, and hold them accountable, you'll be surprised at what gets done. Clear direction, strong leadership, and just the right amount of care can make all the difference in the world.

People are your competitive advantage. They want to win. They want to help you win. All you have to do is create options so they can. Do this, and they'll follow you anywhere.

PULSE CHECK

Empower Yourself

 You may not think you have time to train your people, but the truth is, you don't have time *not* to do it.

 Keep track of the process you use for onboarding new team members so it can be replicated. The prototype is always the most difficult to create. After that, you simply refine it until it's perfect.

Engage Your Team

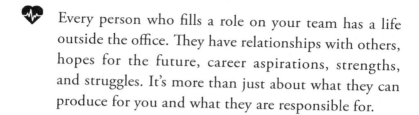 Every person who fills a role on your team has a life outside the office. They have relationships with others, hopes for the future, career aspirations, strengths, and struggles. It's more than just about what they can produce for you and what they are responsible for.

Knowing your people is about who they are as individuals and human beings. When you know what's important to them in life in general, you can tap into what motivates them. It's true that people don't care how much you know until they know how much you care.

Impact Your Organization

Understanding employees' goals and objectives, why they are working for the organization, what's in it for them, and what they want to get out of working for this organization begins by setting realistic expectations.

When it comes to expectations, you can never over-communicate. Tell your employees what you expect. Write it down. Send it in an email. Put it on a whiteboard. Clear expectations require courage from the leader, but they are invaluable to the people they lead.

CHAPTER 8

PULSE 4: PROCESSES

THE DRIVERS OF LEADERSHIP

A lot of people misunderstand processes. They think processes tie their hands or bind them rigidly to a set of rules. But really, nothing could be further from the truth.

Processes—when done correctly—are liberating. They take the guesswork out of repeated day-to-day tasks and help you function on autopilot. They help you minimize the energy you spend on trivial matters so you can focus on what is important. In short, good processes help reduce the *friction* of leadership.

The number-one enemy of leaders or contributors is time. It's finite and always goes faster than you think it will. So regarding time, there are a few questions leaders need to ask themselves if they ever want to streamline their processes:

- How do I *spend my time*?

- How can I make sure I'm getting *the best return* on my time?

- Does the way I spend my time ultimately *drive the results* I want?

I've seen many people work really hard, but they're really not spending their time in the right places. It may be that somebody else is controlling their agenda. They may not have a clear idea of what their priorities are. They may just be a poor manager of time. They may be trying to do too much. Or they may be working in an area that simply isn't their strength.

> TO BE SUCCESSFUL OVER TIME AND TO KEEP YOUR WORKLOAD SUSTAINABLE, YOU MUST HAVE A SYSTEM OR PROCESS FOR GETTING THE RIGHT THINGS DONE.

To be successful over time and to keep your workload sustainable, you must have a system or process for getting the *right* things done. You can't just wing it. Yet, a lot of people wing it every day. It's their preferred method of operation. They sit around waiting for an email to show up in their inbox, for the boss to tell them what to do, or for the phone to ring.

When those things happen, they stay busy for a moment, but then the urgency dies down and they wait for the impromptu process to start all over again. It's not an efficient way to work. And if those things don't happen, they really don't have a plan for the day. No wonder so many people are disengaged and ineffective at work!

CALENDARIZE YOUR SUCCESS

Your process determines how you allocate your time *for* yourself and *to* other people. If you're leading the team well and ensuring that you are effectively focusing on the things that will deliver, you'll achieve the majority of your business results. It's the 80/20 Pareto Principle in action.

Developing good processes starts when you embrace the idea of a routine. For years, I had a routine I brought with me from position to position. I'd adapt it to the specific job, but my routine and I became dear friends. It helped me take the thinking out of certain repeatable tasks to allow them to become automatic.

When I'm coaching clients, one of the first questions I get asked is often *how can I create processes and systems that will help me get my work done without going crazy?* Most things in life are repetitive, and work is no different. If you were to objectively look at your job and your deliverables, you'd probably be able to break it down into a handful of key things to accomplish each day to ensure your days, weeks, and months were a success.

Stephen Covey rightly advised to begin with the end in mind. Many times people struggle to establish processes because they haven't defined a successful ending. If I were to ask you, *At the end of the day, what defines success in your role?* What would you say?

You may look at your to-do list and see how many things you were able to cross off. You may look at your numbers and see if you hit your targets. You may look at the boss's closed office door and figure, *Hey, if the boss is quiet, I must be on track.*

But are any of those really a measure of your success? If you stack day after day like that together, does it lead to where you want to go? Even more telling is this: if I were to look at your daily calendar for the last six months, would the way you spend your time show me that you are effectively moving toward your goal?

For a lot of people, that one hurts. We know we aren't maximizing our time, but because we're busy, we don't stop to discover why. Busyness does not equal productivity.

No one has complete control of their time. There will always be somebody or something which influences your agenda or your calendar. But that doesn't mean you can't optimize the way you spend the time that is yours. And you can only do this when you define success and monitor your key touchpoints.

Touchpoints are the key things you need to have your hands on each day. A lot of leaders make the mistake of wanting to be involved in *everything,* and then they wonder why they're so frazzled at the end of the day. As you rise in leadership, it's not uncommon for you to have a looser grip on the details. You have to fly up to a 30,000-foot level to see it all. That can be a real challenge for the leader who is used to being in the trenches.

The higher I rose up the corporate ladder, the more I had to realize I was responsible for a growing number of stakeholders. As you know by now, I love people and believe in servant leadership. So when I became Zone Sales Manager, every time somebody would come to my office, every time somebody would call me, I would take the call or talk to them in my office. Invariably, my day would fly by. I'd look up at the clock on the wall and see that it was already 5:30. In a panic, I'd look at my calendar and see that nothing I planned to do had been done.

So what did I have to do? I had to go home and do the work that I needed to get done during the day. That works for a short period of time but burns you out very, very quickly. I had to answer the success question, or I wasn't going to be around much longer.

How do I do my work and still be the leader that I want to be? How do I stay accessible to coach and develop my team, yet still get my job done?

After wrestling with these questions, I quickly developed a routine. I had the flexibility to spend two days in the office and three days in the field, and this was a godsend. On Mondays and Tuesdays, I'd be in the office. I'd look at the scorecards for the last week. I'd connect with my key direct reports and my leaders. I'd look at my forecast to understand what was coming up and what activities we should be pursuing. Then from Wednesday on, I was on the road with my teams.

Once I defined success for me, things became much simpler and more focused. I knew the touchpoints that needed my personal attention. I calendarized my priorities because what gets calendarized gets done. Even after I left Frito-Lay and went to Coca-Cola, I advocated keeping the same type of schedule because I could demonstrate the results it brought for the company.

You may not have that exact flexibility, but everybody can create a routine for themselves that maximizes their effectiveness in the key deliverables they are responsible for—even you!

Start with these three questions:

1. What are the optimum conditions for me to get my work done?

2. How do I make sure I'm allocating enough time to the most important things?

3. How do I try to control or minimize distractions from other people on my agenda?

In college, I was very organized. Everything was planned on my calendar. When I got to corporate America, that practice got blown to pieces. Suddenly, I had to be a part of other people's meetings, and things weren't quite so tidy. I became frustrated and thought, *I cannot work like this.* But I realized very quickly that although I could not be too rigid, I couldn't be a "wing-it" person either. The sweet spot was somewhere in the middle. Calendarize the things you have to do to be successful at your job. But then leave flexibility for the interruptions—and there will *always* be interruptions.

> CALENDARIZE THE THINGS YOU HAVE TO DO TO BE SUCCESSFUL AT YOUR JOB. BUT THEN LEAVE FLEXIBILITY FOR THE INTERRUPTIONS—AND THERE WILL ALWAYS BE INTERRUPTIONS.

When I realized this truth, it changed my thinking. Instead of scheduling every moment of my day, I started to determine how much time of my day is ad hoc, filled with unexpected and uncontrollable things that come up. Armed with a general idea of this information, I stopped scheduling every minute of my day because I knew something would come up.

I became more realistic about my calendar and kept a couple of hours of the day open for the unexpected. Planning for the unexpected leaves you plenty of time to do the important. And calendarizing your success ensures that you'll *be* a success. It's the first step towards developing a process that works for you. Find your ideal way to work, then work that way.

MANAGE YOUR LEADER

It may sound crazy, but you also need a process to manage your leader. A lot of people have difficulty standing up to their boss. Now, I *was* the boss for many years, so let me unpack that a bit. Obviously your boss got to where he or she is for a reason. You have to treat your superior with the respect that the title deserves.

So managing your leader isn't about *bossing* your leader around; it's about training your leader how to lead you well. The best way I found to do that was with a weekly or biweekly one-on-one meeting. These weekly one-on-ones can be an invaluable tool to build relational capital that can pay huge dividends in the future. In these sessions, you can foster communication and build rapport. You can also directly and indirectly impact your future.

At the heart of the art of one-on-one is communication. Communication isn't something most people build a process around. They just open their mouths and talk, or wait until something small turns into something big and then scramble to fix a problem. One-on-ones foster communication about the people you lead, the health of your department, questions and concerns, constructive feedback, and career growth goals.

The trick is that most leaders aren't going to invite *you* to a one-on-one meeting. Only the best leaders say, "Welcome to the company! Let's sit down and talk about expectations and how I'm going to measure you." This is why I was such a stickler for onboarding my direct reports. I know that most people never ask their boss the question, *How will you measure my success in this role?*

In your one-on-one with your boss, this is one of the best questions you can ask and use it to branch out into many different directions. It eliminates confusion around your focus on what you think is important while your boss thinks something else is important.

At Coca-Cola, I had a biweekly meeting with my leader. He didn't do it with everybody, but he did it for me *because I asked for it*. It was critical for me to make sure the work I was doing was in alignment with his expectations. It also gave him the opportunity to give me real-time feedback so I could adjust and course-correct when and where necessary. The process of these one-on-ones helped me minimize surprises and maximize where I spent my time.

If you want to set up regular one-on-ones with your leader, you've got to be aware that their time is as compressed as yours. John Maxwell wrote, "Be prepared every time you take your leader's time. A 360-Degree Leader should be ready to ask the right questions and to bring something to the table. Preparation paves the way for both leaders to add value to each other."[9]

I had a simple agenda for most of my one-on-ones. First, I'd cover the issues I believed to be important to *them*. My biggest clues came from three questions that I'd answer before each meeting:

1. What did they interrupt me on since we last met?

2. What did they call me out of the blue about in the past two weeks?

3. What did they send me urgent or important emails about?

These three questions told me a lot about what I need to proactively communicate. Answering these questions first showed that I was in tune with what was important to them and that I took seriously what they took seriously.

After we worked through those things, I would update them on any people issues I was having. We'd discuss the health of the business as well as any results or performance issues I was struggling with. I'd cover the big things I was working on to improve the business.

Next, if I had any questions or concerns, I would ask those at that time. And the last thing I always asked was there any feedback from them or any other key stakeholder.

Over time, one-on-ones develop into something more. You don't have to love your boss to benefit from these meetings, but you will develop a mutual respect for each other. As your eyes are opened to the burdens they face, and they see you as a critical part of the organization, you can both add value to each other and ensure you are moving in the right direction.

BECOME A PROBLEM-SOLVER

No matter how much you try, you'll always run into problems. In fact, solving problems may be the definition of work. The bad news is there will be problems; the good news is if you create a process for solving them and do it often enough, you get a reputation as a problem-solver—and that's a reputation worth having.

> THE BAD NEWS IS THERE WILL BE PROBLEMS; THE GOOD NEWS IS IF YOU CREATE A PROCESS FOR SOLVING THEM AND DO IT OFTEN ENOUGH, YOU GET A REPUTATION AS A PROBLEM-SOLVER—AND THAT'S A REPUTATION WORTH HAVING.

A lot of folks are trying to get their job done *just* within the confines of their department or function, without really understanding the interdependencies between functions and departments. I call these "functional silos" because they may be working hard in their departments, but they aren't building those relationships across the organization that help them effectively solve problems. So how do you build in time to do that?

Pause. The first step to building a problem-solving routine is a bit counterintuitive because it feels like the opposite of action. The first thing you do when you encounter a problem is to *pause*. We're so quick to *do*, but we're much slower to *stop and think*. If you don't make thinking about a problem part of your routine, you'll likely rush to an incomplete solution. Even worse, it may actually solve the wrong problem.

Before you start doing, you must pause long enough to figure out what really needs to be done and whether or not it will actually solve the problem. By rushing to provide a solution, you may think you solved the problem, but in reality, you just kicked the problem down the road.

Consider this. Most companies have a sales department and a delivery department. Suppose your company is getting a repetitive customer complaint that their delivery is late. As a leader, your initial solution is simple. *I'm going to call the delivery manager and tell him this store has to be delivered by eight o'clock every morning.* You hang up the phone and think, *Well, that was easy* and move on to the next thing.

In the warehouse, the delivery manager makes a note on the trip sheet—*make sure customer X gets first delivery.* He shakes his head in half amusement and half frustration because this customer is almost always the first one delivered anyway. But he thinks, *Whatever, you're the boss.*

Everyone moves on, and you forget about the problem... that is until you get another call the next week from the now-angry customer. *Every day last week, my delivery was late!* he screams into the phone. You promise to look into it and call him right back. *I thought I fixed this issue, why is it still a problem?*

You immediately call the delivery manager and ask him what's going on. He tells you to hang on a minute while he grabs his notes from last week's delivery. As you hear papers rustling in the background, you get a sense he knew this call was coming.

Your delivery manager gets back on the line and tells you that he talked to the driver who arrived at the customer's location every day at 7:30 AM, but spent an hour waiting for a dock door to become available. By making this customer the first stop, the driver now spends the most productive part of his day sitting in a traffic jam in the customer's yard.

You thank the delivery manager and hang up. *Hmm,* you think to yourself, *this is a little more complicated than I thought.* Now, you've got to exhibit courageous leadership and call the customer back to explain the problem and try to find a mutually beneficial solution.

What seemed like a slam-dunk fix before could have actually been solved if you'd taken the time to pause, gather the facts, and *then* make a plan.

Be Inquisitive. The next step is to be inquisitive. Ask questions. Look for the cause behind the cause. It's easy to react to a problem based on one person's version of the facts. However, that perspective is rarely all there is to the story. Don't just go strictly into problem-solving before you truly understand the nature of the problem.

> QUESTIONS ARE LIKE CLUES. THE MORE YOU ASK, THE MORE YOU UNDERSTAND.

Nine times out of ten, being a problem-solver takes you out of the scope of your immediate job. Yet often we immediately try to solve the problem *inside* our four walls. Most problems involve somebody else that we don't work with every day. You've got to trace the problem back to its origin, which is not always your department or, as in the case above, even your company. Questions are like clues. The more you ask, the more you understand.

Look for Repetition. An issue that happens once is an anomaly that may not be repeated. An issue that happens over and over again is a problem. Most leaders treat problems like paper cuts. They slap a Band-Aid on it to get it quickly off their desk, but that doesn't solve the problem—at least not for long. It certainly doesn't develop a process for ensuring the problem doesn't happen again.

If you keep having to solve the same issue, it's a problem that will keep coming back. Stop the Band-Aid approach and pause to work through a solution. Knowing and understanding which things are one-offs and which ones are consistent is critical before you move to the final step.

Create a Routine. Anything that is repetitive can be simplified with a routine. This is true for problems, too. To determine where you need a routine, think about these questions: What tends to take you off-course in terms of where you're spending your time? Is it repetitive? If it's the same stuff coming up over and over again, you've got to ask yourself, why is it continuing to come up?

If you aren't willing to get to the root cause of the issue, then you're allowing yourself to be reactionary, and that's just on you. If you discover an ongoing problem that you have yet to solve, then create a process. Establish a problem-solving task force. Brainstorm solutions. Create action plans. Follow up and hold people accountable. Meet weekly until it's fixed.

Discuss the issue once, and then let people work on the solution. Empower people to do their part, then reconnect until it's solved. You can't lose sight of your problems, but you can't allow them to suck away all your time either.

ENGAGE YOUR KEY STAKEHOLDERS

The final thing to consider when it comes to processes is how you manage your key stakeholders. A key stakeholder is anybody that either has direct or indirect interests or impact in your business. In this case, your business is your career. If you want to be a Heartbeat Leader, you've got to intentionally nurture these relationships so they work for you. But it shouldn't be self-serving. You should seek to add value to these relationships.

The best leaders develop a stakeholder map. It can be either formal or informal. The trick is that they look way beyond just their own leaders and direct reports. Many people think way too small when it comes to stakeholders. As I work with my executive coaching clients, whether they have been in the role years or a few months, we end up doing a stakeholder map to unlock solutions to problems and work collaboratively.

People tend to go directly inward and think about what area they are responsible for. That's a great place to start, but it can't be where you finish. When you begin to develop your stakeholder map, get really creative around sketching it out. Think through both up and down the line who touches the business that you are a part of.

Who is upstream that you have to keep close and keep informed or engaged in getting your job done? Of course, your boss is on the list, but what about his boss? What about a VP? You also have to look laterally. Who are your counterparts in other departments? How does your work affect their work and vice versa?

Expand further still. How do other departments you rarely interact with affect your work? Who *outside* of your organization impacts your business? You need a process to manage that interaction as well. Each stakeholder might need resources from up, down, and across the organization, and that affects you.

Once you identify all your key stakeholders (and this process will take some time), you can begin scheduling time for one-on-one conversations. In each new job, I always sat down with my key stakeholders and asked, *How might our departments best work together?* Then I'd ask, *What do you need from my team to be successful in your team?* I'd give them plenty of time to talk and let them know that my intention wasn't for this to be a one-and-done conversation. It was meant to be an ongoing dialogue. Then I'd share what I believed my team would need from theirs in order to be successful.

AS A LEADER, YOUR JOB IS TO REMOVE OBSTACLES.

Those conversations weren't an everyday occurrence. But I would try to invest more time reaching out to build bridges rather than reacting to every urgency that came across my desk.

As a leader, your job is to remove obstacles. You can't do that if you don't have relationships across the company. Those relationships eliminate those functional silos by allowing you to reach out to your counterparts across teams and divisions. If you've never taken the time to get to know these people and an issue arises, it's impossible to form the relationship quickly. They'll look at you like you are a stranger—because you are.

At the end of the day, you can't do for the team what you don't do effectively for yourself. Processes don't need to be constraining or overly labor-intensive. At the core of every process is a desire to streamline your time, simplify your life, and make you a better leader. Processes take the guesswork out of repetitive work and give you the bandwidth to tackle projects where your strengths and abilities make the most impact.

Define your success and work to operate most of the time in that area. Don't let distractions derail you. Don't let busyness distract you from productivity. Get to know your leader, and become a leader your team understands. Give your leader the tools to speak with you, and get clear on his or her expectations and measurements so you are sure you are hitting your targets. Develop a process for solving problems, and you'll become an invaluable resource at every level of your organization. Know and engage your key stakeholders, and it will give you a greater understanding of how the business works and where you and your team can remove obstacles.

James Clear, author of *Atomic Habits: An Easy & Proven Way to Build Good Habits & Break Bad Ones,* puts it this way: "When you fall in love with the process rather than the product, you don't have to wait to give yourself permission to be happy. You can be satisfied anytime your system is running."[10]

Over time, you'll discover that processes are the drivers of your leadership and the system that keeps you running effectively. If you're doing it right, it should filter down to everyone below you.

PULSE CHECK

Empower Yourself

 Calendarize the things you have to do to be successful at your job. But then leave flexibility for the interruptions—and there will *always* be interruptions.

The first thing you do when you encounter a problem is to *pause*. We're so quick to *do*, but we're much slower to *stop and think*.

Request a weekly or biweekly one-on-one meeting with your leader. These weekly one-on-ones can be an invaluable tool to build relational capital that can pay huge dividends in the future.

Engage Your Team

If you discover an ongoing problem that you have yet to solve, create a process. Establish a problem-solving task force. Brainstorm solutions. Create action plans. Follow up and hold people accountable. Meet weekly until it's fixed.

Teach your team members to ask great questions first, before rushing in to "solve" every problem they encounter.

Impact Your Organization

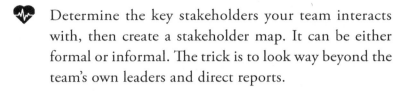 Determine the key stakeholders your team interacts with, then create a stakeholder map. It can be either formal or informal. The trick is to look way beyond the team's own leaders and direct reports.

If you build cross-functional routines, you position your team to impact the organization by being ready to solve complex problems.

As a leader, your job is to remove obstacles. You can't do that if you don't have relationships across the company. Those relationships eliminate functional silos by allowing you to reach out to your counterparts across teams and divisions.

CHAPTER 9

PULSE 5: PERFORMANCE

THE METRICS OF LEADERSHIP

When you think about any job, from the C-Suite down to the frontline worker, there's one measure of success—how well did you execute and produce results? You can do all the other things right, but if you don't create results, you aren't adding to the bottom line.

In some cases, this reality has created leaders who overlook the person and only see what the person *does*. If you've learned anything reading this book, I hope you've learned that's not my recommended approach. You can get results from just about any person, but the *People &* approach takes that performance to the next level.

Pulse 4 was all about *Processes*. Processes are more about *how* to get the right things done efficiently and effectively. Performance is about the *what*—the results themselves. But it's the integration between *how* you do your work, and *what* work you do that actually gets results.

My experience has shown that performance management has always been about the numbers only. What did you produce? What sales did you generate? What costs did you incur? Where did you contribute to overall productivity? These metrics are important, but Heartbeat Leaders have to see *beyond* the numbers to the person *behind* the numbers. A person could get great results but leave dead bodies on the side of the road as they do it. The collateral damage on the sidelines may not hurt in the short-term, but ultimately it will. The Heartbeat Leader cares just as much about *how* they did it as *what* they did.

FORMAL VS. INFORMAL PERFORMANCE MANAGEMENT

Since I left corporate America and began my coaching practice, I've noticed an interesting shift. There used to be a very formal performance management process. Employees knew they would receive a yearly performance review. It was formulaic and often informed a bump in pay and a plan for growth and improvement. Some companies would even do a mid-year review as an additional kind of touchpoint.

Now I see companies moving away from the formal performance management process and adopting an informal approach with more touchpoints to give a form of continuous feedback. In theory, that sounds great, but I'd be lying if I said it didn't make me very nervous. If you are a leader, your team needs your feedback, whether it's once a year or on a touchpoint basis. My fear is that without proper training and proper oversight with checks and balances, leaders will each develop their own system for performance reviews, or worse, just get too busy to do them at all.

I understand the thought process behind moving performance conversations from a specific point in time to an ongoing conversation, which I absolutely agree with, but we still need a process and a framework to guide it. As a Heartbeat Leader, you should be having performance management conversations on an ongoing basis with your team, even if your organization still only does annual reviews.

My approach is exactly the same regardless. As a leader, it doesn't matter what your company's performance management process is—your job is to manage it yourself. You'll have a tremendous impact when you ensure it happens more frequently.

There's an obvious benefit to the employee. They always know where they stand with you, where they can improve, and how they impact the bottom line. Their performance growth can then occur in a steady, systematized way throughout the year, rather than in a rush to cram everything in around performance review time.

But there are also tremendous benefits for you as the leader to give more frequent feedback. For example, by having these periodic reviews, you have a better pulse on the heartbeat of your organization. You clearly understand the status of the business from the viewpoint of each individual.

AS A LEADER, IT DOESN'T MATTER WHAT YOUR COMPANY'S PERFORMANCE MANAGEMENT PROCESS IS—YOUR JOB IS TO MANAGE IT YOURSELF.

People work differently, approach things differently, and interpret you differently. Rather than being frustrated about this, when you do periodic performance reviews, you get to see how these varied perspectives can add invaluable insight. You'll begin to learn that when you really get to know your team, you're able to solve problems more quickly. You're able to understand what's going on, why things are happening, or why they're not happening. You're able to connect what first seems unconnected. Armed with that knowledge, you can head off minor issues that could become huge problems if you only reviewed them once a year.

When you make intentional time to review your team's performance, you get a sense of how they think, how they approach their work, and how they leverage (or fail to leverage) the people around them to achieve their objectives. Routine touchpoints with your team—both direct and indirect reports—through one-on-one conversations can be time-consuming. However, information emerges via periodic, one-on-one dialogue in a way that is impossible in a group or even once a year at an annual performance review.

These periodic meetings also make it easy to exercise what I call *situational leadership*. As you begin to see each person as an individual, you learn which teammate needs more or less of your attention. You can then tailor your leadership to the situation and person. You'll only need to touch base with some people and move on.

Getting to know each of their needs also gives you the ability to appreciate each person's skills and abilities, strengths and opportunities. You can coach people through any performance deficiencies you see before they become too big to address in a way that encourages growth. My core philosophy is that as a leader, your role is to make sure your team delivers. But for your team to deliver, you have to be the person who removes obstacles your team can't remove on their own.

Your job is to ensure you understand their goals and what they're trying to get out of their experience at your organization. Where are they trying to go? What's their next move? What do they aspire to? Training and developing them to do their job with excellence now ensures they are prepared for where they want to go in the future. Your job is to help them get what they want. In that process, you'll get what you want. I've witnessed it firsthand, time and time again.

You've got to tap into *why* they're there. Knowing their motivation becomes the lever that allows you to get the best performance out of your entire team. Here's something to think about: if you're not removing obstacles and developing individuals when you're the leader of that team, then what are you doing?

That's a servant leadership mindset. I may be the boss, but I'm actually there to work for my team. When you take that position, it puts the ownership on you. But a Heartbeat Leader wouldn't have it any other way.

LEAD VS. LAG METRICS

I don't know about you, but I'd much rather be a *leader* than a *lagger*.

That's why I find it so strange that most performance metrics focus on lag—what you did in the past, versus lead—what you can do to achieve your targets in the future.

When you focus on lag metrics, you're looking at results *after the fact*. So by the time you sit down with a team member and have a conversation to look at metrics, what's done is done. Hopefully, you can learn from these numbers, and I do believe you should track your progress, but ultimately you can't change the past.

On the other hand, when you implement lead metrics, you focus on changing the future.

That's another benefit of doing frequent one-on-ones with your team. You can highlight activities that will get the desired outcome. If you only focus on the outcome and not the activities required to get there, you may not be doing the right things or not often enough.

> IF YOU ONLY FOCUS ON THE OUTCOME AND NOT THE ACTIVITIES REQUIRED TO GET THERE, YOU MAY NOT BE DOING THE RIGHT THINGS OR NOT OFTEN ENOUGH.

Quite frankly, most people are conditioned to give excuses when they miss a target. Lag metrics acknowledge the reasons you miss a target, but we also need to ask, *Now that we know why we missed, what has to happen to make sure we don't miss it in the future?*

When I began to implement lead metrics into my performance reviews, it was a bit of culture shock for my team. I had hoped they would take ownership, but the excuses bubbled to the top. *I missed my sales plan because the weather was bad.* Or, *The account didn't run the promo pricing.* Or, *My delivery ran late.*

At the end of the day you've got to learn to control the controllable. You can't control the weather, and you can't control other people—you *can* control you. When it came to targets, I'd encourage my team to implement a "plan plus two" goal. This meant I actually had them increase their definition of success by 2%. That small margin began to make all the difference. It had a similar effect to setting the clock ahead ten minutes to ensure you get there on time.

Something always happens, so if you only plan to the precise number, you're usually going to miss it. As a leader, you have to be tough enough to say, *No more excuses. We're going to look at our targets and break them down into manageable pieces.*

As I rose in leadership, I discovered something interesting. We had massive sales plans at the highest levels with huge organization-wide goals. As a vice president, I knew the number my team had to hit to be a success. I made sure my directors knew what their numbers were. But from there, things got a little fuzzy.

When it finally got to the people who actually executed at the front line, they didn't have a granular number to know how to be successful. They had a monthly number, but how do you hit a monthly number?

> PERFORMANCE MANAGEMENT IS NOT ABOUT A SINGLE POINT IN TIME. IT IS NOT A SPECIFIC EVENT, IT'S A PROCESS.

So I gathered my team. We formulated a plan to break those big numbers down into manageable goals. Months are made up of weeks, and weeks are made up of days. We broke the big numbers from corporate into four equal parts. At the end of each week, you'd know you were behind if you weren't at 25% of the way to your target. The idea was to keep that specific goal front and center and for all of the metrics to *lead* them to success. We didn't have to wait for a quarterly scorecard to tell us how we were doing—at the end of every week, we already knew.

Performance management is not about a single point in time. It is not a specific event, it's a process. It has to be in the DNA of what you do each and every day. Everybody has to have a performance management mindset. *We're all here to perform. We're all here to get an end result. What we do is important, but how we do it is also important.*

In the same way that intentionally seeking out your team for periodic one-on-ones requires adjustments, implementing lead metrics also shakes up your culture. High-performance teams deliver over and over and over again. Not just once, but every time. Create a high-performance team, and you create sustainable results.

HOLD PEOPLE ACCOUNTABLE

Have you ever seen a parent with a misbehaving toddler? The parent may plead, beg, warn, and bribe, but the behavior doesn't change. In fact, it seems like things only get worse. Now, I'm not knocking parents. I've been there with two of my own.

But if you continually threaten discipline, even after clearly setting expectations, but then don't hold the person accountable, who's really to blame for bad behavior?

The same principle applies when it comes to performance metrics. When does coaching stop and the introduction of consequences start? Heartbeat Leaders have to walk the line between compassion and consequences. Between coaching and correction. When people aren't making measurable progress and commitments aren't being kept, it's time to hold people accountable. Remember, your goal as a leader is to help make your team better in all areas, including having honest and sometimes difficult conversations.

If you've coached and coached people, but have seen no change in behavior, you must hold people accountable. The process is fairly simple *if* you are willing to execute it.

Follow up and follow through. Leaders tend to drop the ball here more than anywhere. What I find is leaders have initial conversations regarding performance but fail to follow up or follow through. Without following up, you're leaving that behavior change to chance. And even the most sincere employees can quickly backslide into bad habits.

Following up and following through isn't about ruling with an iron fist or being a micromanager who's always watching or leaning over shoulders. It's about setting clear expectations—and that includes a plan for periodic check-ins to monitor progress.

Here's an example. Let's say I'm your leader, and you've struggled to meet your target in some area. So you and I have a conversation about performance. You tell me why you think you've missed your targets, and I offer my observations for what I've seen. After we clear the air, we set some new expectations. After some back and forth, you agree there are certain activities you need to focus on. You agree to implement the plan we just laid out. I ask if you have any questions. You say you don't. You tell me you don't foresee any obstacles to prevent you from starting the first stage of the plan. You promise it will be done by next Thursday.

As a leader, I can't leave it to chance at this point. If it was important enough to have the conversation in the first place, then I've got to follow through. So next Thursday, two things should be happening. You should have sent a proactive communication to me that what I asked is done, or, at a minimum, giving a status update. If by the end of the day on Thursday I haven't received word, then it's up to me to reach out to you to check your status.

This accountability check has to become your process with the people you lead, or time may pass with no improvement. If you've implemented bimonthly one-on-ones, for example, then you might cover items like the one I described in the next meeting.

I just want to reiterate—the goal is not to be a domineering boss who wields power over direct reports. The goal is to help each of them become better, which makes the entire team better. Over the course of my career, I inherited many people who'd been written off as not having much hope for performance improvement. The previous leader had slammed the door shut and been content with C-minus performance.

Time and time again, I'd meet with the person and discuss expectations and problems in achieving them. After we set up a plan for improvement, I'd hold them accountable. Nine times out of ten, their performance improved—and team morale with it.

I believe that you should *inspect* what you *expect*. When people figure out you're not really checking in, they're going to procrastinate on it. That's just human nature. But when people know you are following up, they're going to give it their best shot to get better.

Development or discipline? There's an important question every Heartbeat Leader keeps in mind when conducting performance assessments: is this a *deficiency of skill* or a *deficiency of will*? In other words, do they not know how to do their job or do they just not care enough to do the job? The distinction is huge and sets the tone for how you approach the next steps.

It is the leader's job to differentiate between the two. Deficiency of skill involves development. Deficiency of will requires discipline.

If someone knew what to do, but simply didn't do it, that's clearly a discipline issue. If they have the right tools and the capabilities to do the job, and still aren't getting it done, then you need a performance improvement plan. Either they're going to step it up, or they're going to step out.

But if they didn't know how to do the job, that's an opportunity to equip them for the next time. There's more grace for deficiency of skill than there is for deficiency of will. When I talk to leaders having trouble with performance management and accountability, I always ask them if they are struggling because they haven't identified which deficiency they are facing. We all want to think the best of people, but sometimes you've got to be honest with yourself about their capabilities, attitude, and potential.

When it comes to performance, the best way to help people improve is to go into their environments and observe. Listen in on a sales call and give feedback. If you see they have trouble handling objections, give them ideas for how to handle those objections. When you observe how people do their jobs, you can help them become better.

Be the kind of leader who has their best interests in mind, and let them know it. No one who genuinely wants to improve will have an issue with you helping and observing.

Make feedback an ongoing conversation. Heartbeat Leaders occupy an interesting space. On one hand, as a leader, they are responsible for results, and those results only come when they have their people in the right seat on the bus, working in their area of strength with feedback for continuous improvement. On the other hand, a Heartbeat Leader genuinely cares about their people and wants to temper honesty with kindness and truth with humility.

> THE WAY YOU INTERACT WITH YOUR TEAM COMMUNICATES YOUR HEART.

The way you interact with your team communicates your heart. Your care gets noticed most clearly in the way you give feedback and have ongoing conversations. If you're not walking among your people, having regular conversations, then it can feel risky for your team to be open and honest with you. However if you, as the boss, are somebody they meet once a month and have regular conversations with, then feedback just becomes an offshoot of that. Leaders shouldn't be feared. It's less scary when a direct report knows that you're trying to work *together* toward making things better and improving performance.

You may recall the expression I used earlier: *the audio needs to match the video*. The only way to know if the audio is matching the video with your team is to go see it for yourself. If they don't align, then you can question, offer observations, and share feedback.

ONE OF THE BEST QUESTIONS YOU CAN ASK OF YOUR TEAM IS THIS: WHAT SUPPORT DO YOU NEED FROM ME?

Not just once. Many times, we say we've got to give feedback like it's a one-time event. But feedback is an ongoing conversation. It's a normal part of the interaction between leader and employee. And by the way, it should be *two-way* feedback—not just you doing all the talking.

So many times when I talk to employees who have a difficult leader or don't feel comfortable with their leader, they tell me they don't feel like they can initiate some of these conversations. Knowing that a lot of people are intimidated by a leader's title, I tried to bend over backward to be open and approachable. Yet I still found people sometimes wouldn't be honest or open with me. To make it easier, I asked them the questions, so I didn't force them to *initiate* feedback with me. Questions open dialogue that might otherwise remain closed.

One of the best questions you can ask of your team is this: *What support do you need from me?* I found that this question made it easier for my team to ask for help.

At the end of the day, the boss is still the boss, so you know you will always have the upper hand. That's why your job as a leader is to continue to make it easier for your team to talk to you. If asking them the question and inviting them into the conversation helps them, then you've done your job well. Unfortunately, many leaders take the opposite approach: *Well, you didn't ask me for help or say you were having a problem.*

But think about it. Most people won't walk up to their leader and say, *I'm really struggling with this job (which you are paying me to know how to do). Can you help me?* But if the leader asks where he or she can support that person, people are usually more willing to share and feel safe to answer. They'll even be willing to receive your tough but fair feedback.

LEAD TO HELP PEOPLE SUCCEED

I believe everybody deserves a chance. Think about an underperforming player on a sports team who is traded to another team. Suddenly, that player has a breakout season and looks like a totally different athlete. What changed, the person or their surroundings? The potential was always there, but sometimes it takes a new coach to bring it out.

If you have some underperforming players on your team, what do you need to do to help make them better? An underperformer doesn't always mean writing them off. That is never your first response as a Heartbeat Leader. Your first response should always be to find the root cause.

Remember, there's a person under the performance.

Performance management is a critical piece of Heartbeat Leadership. It takes into account the person and pushes them just enough to bring out their best. When you make it a point to really get to know your team and understand where each person might struggle, you can tailor your leadership to the individual. This approach also gives you a pulse of the organization from people who see things differently than you.

By building lead metrics into your leadership style, you empower your people to identify the right activities that lead to the desired results. Activities are controllable; outcomes are not. Increase the right activities, and you will increase the desired results. Outcome follows activities, and breaking big goals down into smaller milestones can engage and inspire your team.

Accountability and feedback are critical for performance. People will perform up (or down) to your expectations. Expect excellence and give feedback so they can execute well. If you develop a team of high-performers, you improve everything in the organization. Wherever they land, you've given them the skills to succeed.

And that's a mark of a Heartbeat Leader.

PULSE CHECK

Empower Yourself

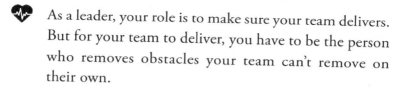

As a leader, your role is to make sure your team delivers. But for your team to deliver, you have to be the person who removes obstacles your team can't remove on their own.

If you're not helping remove obstacles for your team members and not helping them develop to the next level, *you are overhead.* They can do without you.

Engage Your Team

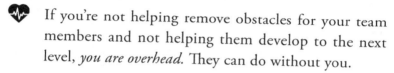

When it comes to targets, encourage your team to implement a "plan plus two" goal. This means to actually have them increase their definition of success by 2%. That small margin makes all the difference.

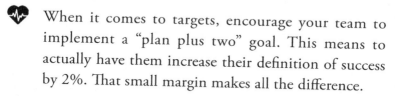

Walk the line between compassion and consequences. Between coaching and correction. When people aren't making measurable progress and commitments aren't being kept, it's time to hold people accountable. Remember, your goal as a leader is to help make your team better in all areas, including having honest and sometimes difficult conversations.

The goal is not to be a domineering boss who wields power over direct reports. The goal is to help each of them become better, which makes the entire team better.

Impact Your Organization

 There's an important question to keep in mind when conducting performance assessments: is this a *deficiency of skill* or a *deficiency of will*? In other words, do they not know how to do their job, or do they just not care enough to do the job? The distinction is huge. Deficiency of skill involves development. Deficiency of will requires discipline.

 Feedback is not a one-time event; it is an ongoing conversation. It's a normal part of the interaction between leader and employee. And by the way, it should be *two-way* feedback—not just the leader doing all the talking.

CHAPTER 10

PULSE 6: PROMOTION

THE GROWTH OF LEADERSHIP

If you're a leader for any length of time, it won't take long to discover something—someone is *always* upset about not being where they thought they should be in their career. Sometimes that someone is you. It may be people feel stuck and can't seem to get promoted. They may want to work in a different department. Sometimes they were frustrated at one company and left to work at another where they thought their chances for advancement were better.

It's not always a case of *the grass being greener on the other side* mentality either. Sometimes there are legitimate reasons for this feeling.

So how do you promote yourself in a way that doesn't seem self-serving? How do you map out a path for your future and your career that is authentic to you and gives you a sense of agency and ownership?

It starts with realizing you have options.

A lot of people feel stuck, but I'm the ultimate optimist. I don't ever feel like you're so stuck you can't move. There are always options. The question is do you want to exercise them? And are you willing to do the hard work to make them pay off? It's not about whether or not you have options; it's about whether or not you want to do anything with the options you have.

> IT'S NOT ABOUT WHETHER OR NOT YOU HAVE OPTIONS; IT'S ABOUT WHETHER OR NOT YOU WANT TO DO ANYTHING WITH THE OPTIONS YOU HAVE.

You may be comfortable where you are, or you might feel like you are trapped. You may be just starting out in leadership and wanting to make sure you have a plan for where you want to go. You may be fifteen years into your career and realizing you're heading in a direction you don't want to go.

Wherever you are, it's much better to take ownership of your own future rather than leaving it up to chance. When you leave your future up to chance, you'll find yourself in a place where you didn't intend to be. You'll miss out on the continuity and authenticity that ties your life and work together. You'll end up unfulfilled. You won't be utilizing your strengths—in fact, you may be working out of an area of weakness, which is always a recipe for disaster.

If you want to avoid a future like this (and let's be honest, no one wants this for their career), you've got to recognize that you have a voice and use it. It's good to be humble, but that doesn't mean you have to be invisible.

For me, from day one, I've always had a clear understanding of what I wanted, my goals and objectives, and where I hoped to go in the organization. With that in mind, I eventually realized that *knowing* what I wanted was only half the battle. I also needed to make sure I knew how to get where I wanted to go. Even more than that, I had to make sure *other* people knew where I wanted to go.

This meant my plan couldn't just stay locked inside my head. It had to be developed there, but it also had to be shared with the people around me. And that meant learning to speak up (which hasn't been too much of an issue for me!), step up to the challenges, and step out in confidence as I demonstrated why I deserved to be the leader I hoped to become.

CHART YOUR COURSE

Imagine someone told you they'd pay for an all-expenses-paid trip to send you to climb Mt. Kilimanjaro in Tanzania. So you do a little research to learn what you'll need to make the journey. Of course, you'll need a passport just to get there. You'll also need the proper equipment to make the journey. At 19,341 feet, it's the highest freestanding mountain in the world. There are five main routes to the top, so you'd have to know which one to take. Once at the top, you'd encounter temperatures right around zero degrees Fahrenheit, so you'd want warm clothes. And good hiking boots would be a must.

Now imagine you did none of that. You simply took your free trip, hopped on the next plane to Africa, and set out for the top of the highest summit on the continent with just the clothes on your back and the contents in your pockets.

How far do you think you'd make it? Probably not that far!

That's how a lot of people approach their career. They see the summit, but they have no plan for how to reach the top. They don't know what their strengths are. They aren't honest about their weaknesses. They simply strike out on the closest path and hope it leads to the top.

If you want to get serious about reaching your career goals, you've got to be honest with yourself. You've got to get clear on what you want and then examine what it takes to get there. From a leadership perspective, one of the best ways to get good feedback is with a 360 leadership assessment. By learning how the people above you, beside you, and beneath you experience your leadership, you can begin to examine what you need to reach your summit.

Sometimes we are better in our own heads than what everybody else thinks. Careful examination provides a litmus test to show where you lead well, where you need to improve, and any blind spots you might be missing. These assessments require humility, vulnerability, and courage, but they help you quantify or validate your strengths and identify potential weaknesses that need to be shored up.

Most of all, to get where you need to go, you need a growth mindset—a willingness to ask the tough questions where a fixed mindset will not. A growth mindset is one of constant course correction, and that's what it takes to be a Heartbeat Leader.

Early in my career at Frito-Lay, Inc. I had my eyes on only one job—Zone Sales Leader. That was the first level of an executive role, and I always had dreams of leading a large team and being responsible for a big business. I didn't know how long it was going to take me to get there, but I knew if I kept my eyes on the goal, I'd get there eventually.

I didn't realize it at first, but this lens became the filter through which I viewed my next jobs. I would always ask myself, *How does this help me get to my ultimate job as a zone sales leader?* I didn't waste any time taking jobs that weren't going to help me move in that vertical direction to that job. That's not to say I loved every job along the way. There were some jobs that I didn't like at all, even though the people in those roles made it worthwhile.

Reaching that job ended up taking me ten years. And there were points in time where I felt like *it shouldn't be taking me this long*, but at the end of the day, every job that I did made me a stronger, better, and more effective Zone Sales Leader. I had cross-functional experience most people in the position didn't have because they had only come up through the sales ranks.

> IDEALLY, YOU SHOULD WANT TO BUILD EXPERIENCES AND SKILLS—NOT JOB TITLES. THOSE ARE TWO COMPLETELY DIFFERENT THINGS.

Sometimes to get to your next job, you've got to move sideways before you move up. When you are mapping out your career track, don't just look straight up. It's not a ladder. It's more of a twisting path that moves up, down, and sideways. Ideally, you should want to build experiences and skills—not job titles. Those are two completely different things.

When I coach people now, I urge them to think about the *skills* they need to do the job. That's why, although about 50% of my moves were lateral, I took those positions gladly because I knew they'd help shape me into a better leader.

This approach was drastically different from most of my peers. They saw one way to the top and plowed ahead in that direction. It made for some frustration when they encountered resistance or got stuck because they had no way to learn the skills they were lacking.

Ironically, I started a trend where taking the cross-functional career path became the preferred route to executive leadership. Several people after me took that same path. If you truly want to become a Heartbeat Leader, you have to remember that everything you do has the potential to impact someone else. People matter. Your leadership can set the tone for those who come behind you. Sometimes it takes a trailblazer to chart a new course.

A lot of my peers stayed in jobs for long periods of time. I was an anomaly because I didn't sit in the jobs for a long period of time, but I did *more* jobs to get there. No matter who you are, whether it's for your personal growth or whether it's for you as a leader trying to help your team get to where they want to go, the same steps apply.

So many times, somebody on your team is frustrated or getting impatient because they're not being promoted yet, but maybe they're knocking the current job out of the park. As a leader, you've got to figure out how to help them.

If you can't get them there, you run the risk of them getting so frustrated they leave your organization and go to another. Great leaders help them develop the skills they still lack by finding projects for them that stretch them and help them grow. They scale their current job and give them a little more responsibility so that they can shine—because they have increased their abilities. The worst thing is somebody who feels like they're stagnant, who feels like they can get no more from the job that they're in, and aren't able to go anywhere else.

> YOUR NUMBER-ONE JOB AS A LEADER (WHETHER THE ORGANIZATION TELLS YOU THIS OR NOT) IS TO DEVELOP OTHER PEOPLE.

Your job as a leader is to figure out how to continue to develop them where they are, whether by giving them special projects or getting them some exposure across the organization on some cross-functional teams. There's a ton of things you can creatively do to keep that person growing and learning while they contribute in the job they're in—and retain them in the meantime.

Be a catalyst. Help coach them to figure out what they want. Become an advocate when the time is appropriate; be their cheerleader and sometimes their sponsor.

Here's the best part. As you manage your relationships with those above you in the organization, you'll be able to really convey what your team members want, and *that* makes you look good. Your number-one job as a leader (whether the organization tells you this or not) is to develop other people.

Looking back, I can see that all of my promotions were *a result of being focused on developing others.* I wasn't even looking to be promoted half the time. Sure, I had my goals, but I was more focused on helping other people be better in their jobs. When they got better, it automatically made me look better as well, because I was the leader that led them to grow.

When you focus on other people first, your personal agenda generally takes care of itself.

ADVOCATE FOR YOURSELF

Sometimes, though, the passive approach isn't enough. Sometimes, promotion means learning to fight for yourself. Many times we give our power away to the organizations we work for. We can allow ourselves to become cogs in the wheel, and that makes us think we have no control over our career path.

If you want to take your leadership to the next level, you've got to be willing to advocate for yourself. When things are not going the way you had hoped, don't leave it to someone else to speak for you. Make sure the people that need to know your story know where you're trying to go.

I've sat in the rooms where people are discussing succession planning. A name will pop up for an open position, and one person in the room says, *No they don't want to do that job* or *They're not relocatable.* Somebody else in the room says, *Well, that's not what they told me.*

Now there are different sets of stories, and neither comes from the person being discussed! If that's you they are discussing, it means they're going to make decisions based on what they believe to be true at that moment. Maybe you miss out on the opportunity because it wasn't clear what you wanted, or they didn't really know what your intentions were.

Most organizations have what they call talent management profiles. These are the things that you put out on the company's intranet or with HR about what your interests are, your history and other pertinent details. As a leader looking to fill a position, I found that for a lot of people, these were often incomplete. It made it difficult to sort through the names to see who would be a good fit.

In my career, I always made sure those types of documents were updated and had my latest desires and wishes. I also took the time to share my latest accomplishments. As they say, it's not bragging if you can back it up. If you're serious about getting to the next level, leverage all the tools at your disposal.

EMBRACE YOUR OPPORTUNITIES

In 2016, I had an opportunity to take some of my own advice. Coca-Cola Refreshments was entering into a restructuring phase, and that meant downsizing. Around the teams I worked with there was a lot of anxiety. Naturally, employees were trying to understand where they might land after the dust settled. Would they have a job? Would they get the pink slip? Everything was up in the air for all of us, including me.

It was interesting that amidst all of that I had a sense of peace, because I knew I had options. People would remark on my coolness and ask me why I wasn't worried. I'd tell them, *Because I know I have options.*

These options didn't just come to me overnight. I'd spent my whole career getting ready for something like this. So when it came, I knew my options. As far as I could tell, I had four:

❤ *Option 1:* Ride this out until the very end, and then go work somewhere else.

❤ *Option 2:* Stay and explore other opportunities at Coke.

❤ *Option 3:* Leave now, and go to work for another company.

❤ *Option 4:* Stay to the end, and then go work for myself.

Because I felt like I had options, I was no longer controlled by the uncertainty of what the organization was going to do. All I needed to know was what they were doing, when they were doing it, and how that impacted the four options on the table.

Again, this take was vastly different than what my peers were doing. Many people were waiting for the options to be presented to them. I had created my own options and was leveraging the information around them to figure out which one to activate.

For twenty-six years I worked for two organizations, yet I can't even count how many times I was approached by a headhunter. I answered every headhunter call I ever got and interviewed at every opportunity. Even though I didn't have any inclination of making a change at that moment, I knew that part of advocating for myself was understanding my market worth and practicing my interview skills.

I wanted to build relationships in other industries and know without a doubt that I was valuable outside the organization. One time I was able to leverage another company's interest in me for a huge pay increase. I also wanted to be able to help others who might be looking for a job. Because I had relationships with headhunters, I'm always sending my list of quality names of colleagues to the headhunters and the headhunters' names to colleagues. Even now, on the other side of my corporate career, I still get calls from people who are looking for good people. Since my heart still beats for my people, I gladly share names.

> **HEARTBEAT LEADERS TAKE CHARGE OF THEIR OWN CAREERS.**

A lot of people feel some kind of weird loyalty or doubt that it's dishonest to develop these relationships. I was very loyal (two organizations in twenty-six years, remember), but I also always had a Plan B in case something happened.

You can't wait for change to happen. In this day, and especially if you're middle-aged, it is not about *if*, it's about *when* the restructuring or downsizing is going to happen. It's not necessarily right, but it happens. So don't wait for that day and then try to figure out what you're going to do. Be ready. That way if you need your plan, you know what to do, who to talk to, what companies may be a good fit, and who to call. You know your value, and you're not afraid to test the waters and bet on yourself.

You also need to be thinking of how you are positioning your people for success. Your true test of leadership is your ability to develop others and export talent to other parts of the organization. Being actively involved in the performance management processes is key: ensure your team has active development plans in place that are reviewed regularly, understand the career aspirations of all your employees, and have an active succession plan in place for each of your positions.

Knowing you personally have options is empowering and makes you better at your current job. When your value has been independently quantified, it is a confidence booster. When you've talked to somebody else, or when you've gone on that interview and held your own, it's empowering. It's a better thing all around because you're not playing scared.

You're playing confident.

Interestingly enough, I was offered 95% of the jobs I interviewed for that I didn't necessarily even want. A couple of them were tempting, but I ultimately stayed put. Testing the market also helps you refine your vision for what you want by showing you what you *don't* want. Don't be so comfortable that you don't even explore other opportunities.

One of the best ways to get noticed is to make sure you have a complete LinkedIn profile. It's a powerful tool that has the ability to connect you to other people. Now, my profile is almost my complete resume. Be sure to keep your LinkedIn profile current with what you are working on, what you are learning, and plenty of testimonials from people you've served well.

If you do your job well and are worth talking about, the right people will find you. When you make those connections, you learn that leadership really is people-first. And when you begin to make the Six Pulses of Heartbeat Leadership your mantra and your methodology, being known as a great leader becomes a byproduct.

PURSUE YOUR FUTURE

The best way to avoid feeling frustrated and stuck is to plan your own future. Don't just let it come to you. Take charge. Don't simply be a piece on a chessboard where people move you around like a pawn. When it's all said and done, that game will end in checkmate, and you'll be left unfulfilled.

Here's the question you should continually be asking yourself: *How do I leverage all of my experiences from what I'm doing now to get me closer to what I want to do in the future?* You get to choose whether or not you work in vain.

So many people are devastated when they get let go because they just didn't see it coming. They got so ingrained into just working and getting it done (whatever *it* is) that they didn't think about one very important thing. *What you are doing now should always be a platform for what you want to do going forward.* When you do so much in the name of work, you forget about what it can do for you personally if you are intentional.

So, here's the questions for you now: What is it you want for your future? Does what you are doing now match with what you want to do in the future?

If you want your future to be bright, you've got to mine your present for every lesson it can teach you. You've got to discover what you can learn from your current job to leverage in the future. You need to use what you don't like now to frame where you'll get the greatest enjoyment in the days and years to come.

Discover those things you can transfer out of your current experience to the rest of your life.

Everything I did had a method behind it. I was going somewhere, and I wasn't going to stop until I got there. You own your career, and along with it your leadership journey. If you have a passion for something, leverage your current company needs to develop it. I developed my passion for speaking because I ended up doing it as part of my job. If you have a weakness, ask for honest feedback so you can improve. If you have a particular strength, make sure that everyone knows about it and back it up with results. Develop the transferable skills that will help you for the rest

> **HERE'S THE QUESTION YOU SHOULD CONTINUALLY BE ASKING YOURSELF: HOW DO I LEVERAGE ALL OF MY EXPERIENCES FROM WHAT I'M DOING NOW TO GET ME CLOSER TO WHAT I WANT TO DO IN THE FUTURE?**

of your life, and pretty soon they'll speak louder for you than you ever could.

When your heartbeat is for helping others and your track record shows it, your leadership—and your life—will change in ways you can't imagine.

PULSE CHECK

Empower Yourself

💓 If you don't take ownership of your career, you'll end up unfulfilled. You won't be utilizing your strengths—in fact, you may be working out of an area of weakness, which is always a recipe for disaster.

💓 You've got to recognize that you have a voice and use it. It's good to be humble, but that doesn't mean you have to be invisible.

💓 Make sure you know how to get where you want to go. Even more than that, make sure *other* people know where you want to go.

💓 From a leadership perspective, one of the best ways to get good feedback is with a 360 leadership assessment. By learning how the people above you, beside you, and beneath you experience your leadership, you can begin to examine what you need to reach your career goals.

💓 Always have a Plan B in case something happens. In this day, and especially if you're middle-aged, it is not about *if,* it's about *when* the restructuring or downsizing is going to happen. So don't wait for that day and then try to figure out what you're going to do. Be ready.

Engage Your Team

 Although somebody on your team may be frustrated or getting impatient because they're not being promoted yet, maybe they're knocking the current job out of the park. As a leader, you've got to figure out how to help them get there. Your job as a leader is to figure out how to continue to develop them where they are, whether by giving them special projects or getting them some exposure across the organization on some cross-functional teams.

Impact Your Organization

 Your true test of leadership is your ability to develop others and export talent to other parts of the organization. Being actively involved in the performance management processes is key: ensure your team has active development plans in place that are reviewed regularly; understand the career aspirations of all your employees, and have an active succession plan in place for each of your positions.

CONCLUSION

There's no test quite like leaving one organization—where you had devoted the past twenty or so years of your life—for another, to see if your leadership principles hold true and can be applied in a new place with new people and a new culture. Add a major reorganization to the mix in the new role, and you've got the perfect crucible where *everything* you believe can be tested and refined.

That's exactly what happened to me when I joined Coca-Cola Enterprises. Already a heavyweight in the industry, the Coca-Cola Company was purchasing the largest bottler in North America. As a result of the reorganization that followed the acquisition, I ended up taking a different role than the one I interviewed for initially.

Fortunately, I've always been able to roll with the punches, so while I thought I was going in as a Market Unit Vice President, instead they created a new role for me. This new role would be sort of a holding place until the final reorganization was complete. I was now joining Coke as Vice President, Sales and Operations Planning.

I really wanted to get back to Chicago, but of course, there was no guarantee that would happen. And I would *never* have dreamed in a million years the events that would unfold and take me back to Chicago to become the Market Unit Vice President.

Sadly, it was the kind of day I can never forget.

The leadership transition team was all gathered in Chicago for a two-day meeting. It was chaotic but productive and had me looking forward to the challenges ahead. At the end of the first day, I pulled the current Market Unit Vice President of Chicago aside for a conversation. I wanted to learn all I could about his role and the Chicago market itself as part of my onboarding. He graciously agreed to set up some time with me in the coming week to talk in more detail.

That was the last conversation we ever had.

The morning of the second day of the meeting started as it normally would. Most of us came in, grabbed our coffee, sampled a few pastries, and settled into our seats. We sat there waiting for the meeting to begin, but soon started to realize something was going on. The senior leadership team was nowhere to be found. After about thirty minutes, our Business Unit Leader came in and walked to the front of the room. You could tell by his body language that he was emotionally drained. He called us to attention and, since there's no good way to deliver bad news, just poured out the truth—our colleague, the Chicago Market Unit Vice President, the man I'd been talking to just about fifteen hours ago in this very room and looking forward to learning from in the coming weeks—had been killed in a train accident.

I couldn't believe it. I felt like I'd been punched in the chest. My heart sank to the floor, and tears rolled down my face. I looked to the corner of the room where I had just spoken with him the night before. It didn't seem real.

The rest of the day was a blur.

But for the rest of us, life had to go on.

After a couple of months had passed, we quickly approached the date which would transition us from Coca-Cola Enterprises to Coca-Cola Refreshments. No announcement had been made yet about who was going to fill the void and be named the new Market Unit Vice President of Chicago.

It's funny how shifting circumstances can change your perspective. Heartbeat Leadership is emotional leadership. Three months prior, I'd been *wanting* to go to Chicago. Now, I was thinking, "Please don't ask me to go to Chicago."

The previous leader was *very* well respected and loved. The wounds of his loss were still too fresh in my mind. And I'd only known him for a short while. I could only imagine how the people who worked closely with him were feeling. It would be a daunting task for the next leader to fill that empty spot. In addition, the Coca-Cola culture was one that highly valued tenure and working your way up through the organization. I had industry experience but was brand new at Coke.

Of course, the phone call I was worried about came— *Dawn, we would like to extend an offer for you to become the new Market Unit Vice President for Chicago.* This is what I was hoping for when I joined the organization, but I didn't want to assume the role under *these* conditions.

It was time to make a decision once again—I knew that if I applied all I had learned about Heartbeat Leadership to this new role, then I could bring its message to people who were confused, hurting, and uncertain about the future. That alone would be worth it. It would be my biggest challenge yet; I had big shoes to fill, and I was facing a significant amount of organizational transformation at the same time.

The challenge started the moment I did. In the first two weeks of the role, I had to contact people I hadn't even met and inform them that they no longer had a job. These were difficult conversations, but I was determined to live out my *People &* ideal even on these phone calls. They were people *and* they had been through a lot. I tried to be as compassionate as I could on each and every call.

Internally, I had to pick my entire leadership team with no more information than what I could find on flip charts on the wall and the recommendations of my new colleagues.

Externally, I was preparing to sell my house in Michigan, buy one in Chicago, and physically get everything moved by December 31st in time for my kids to start at their new school before the second semester.

They say leadership is truly defined in the uncomfortable or stressful moments. I was nothing but stressed and uncomfortable, but I leaned on the Six Pulses of Leadership™ to navigate very intentionally in this role.

Here's what I learned:

Pulse 1—Priorities: There was no lack of priorities at Coca-Cola. In fact, it was a running joke that we had so many priorities, you didn't know which priority to prioritize. I quickly distilled my leadership priorities into three main buckets:

1. Onboard quickly to gain the trust of the team.
2. Design and stand up the new organization quickly.
3. Get back to the basics of blocking and tackling the day-to-day business to stabilize the uncertainty.

These *Priorities* gave *Purpose* to my leadership.

Pulse 2—Preparation: Because we were going through a significant transformation, it was important that I was well-versed on all the changes. I had to prepare for their impacts on both individuals and teams. As a leader, I had to keep a pulse on the morale of the team. I extensively prepared in advance for every conference call, townhall, 1-to-1 meeting, and leadership meeting to make sure I was sharing the key messages and ensuring we were all on the same page.

This *Preparation* provided the *Energy* for my leadership.

Pulse 3—People: I invested a lot of time talking with people at each level of the organization to get to know them personally, so I could understand their career goals and aspirations. To get insight into the culture and morale, I always asked three core questions:

1. What's working?
2. What's not working?
3. What do you need from me to do your job better?

We put tremendous focus on the core people processes of onboarding, development plans, and recognition. In my opinion, the recognition that made the biggest impact was recognition of service anniversaries, special events in their lives, and sending holiday cards to every employee.

My *People* became the *Power* of my leadership.

Pulse 4—Process: Because there were so many moving parts, I had to establish routines quickly to keep the lines of communication open. I established one-to-ones with my direct reports weekly and sometimes daily. We set up weekly staff meetings, monthly cross-functional team meetings, and a host of listening sessions and town hall meetings from the top down to the frontline.

These *Processes* became the *Drivers* of my leadership.

Pulse 5—Performance: To understand how I needed to measure success, I dug into the P&L to understand how we were performing and how the plan was constructed. Then I worked to ensure my team understood this as well. I worked hand-in-hand with my finance team to create sales plans from the top levels to the frontline teams.

This approach dramatically changed our performance trajectory. We went from missing targets the first six months of my tenure to surpassing those targets the last six months of our first year. Another game-changer was partnering with my operations counterparts to ensure we understood how we impacted one another. This allowed us to take a very balanced approach that became a driver of profitable growth.

Our *Performance* served as the *Metrics* of my leadership.

Pulse 6—Promotion: My number-one strategy for promoting my team was through the talent review process. Previously, this process and conversation only presided at the highest levels of the organization. I replicated it through *all the levels* of my organization.

This strategy allowed me to get to know my entire organization better; it developed my team's skills in talent management, and it created trust and transparency around why certain people were promoted and what it would take for any person to move to the next level. We made a big deal out of all promotions by sending out formal announcements to celebrate successes.

This *Promotion* strategy translated to the *Growth* of my leadership.

I can tell you from personal experience, the Six Pulses of Leadership™ work! There is no way I would have been successful in transitioning from Frito-Lay to Coca-Cola without this people-first approach. Out of all the roles I've held in my career, this by far was my favorite. Despite all the challenges, we accomplished a lot as a team in a short two-and-a-half years.

IT COMES DOWN TO YOU

When it comes to Heartbeat Leadership, there are two things to keep in mind—people are the heartbeat of your organization, and when it comes to leadership, you have to choose to take ownership of your journey.

The heart health of your people depends on you. Not the people you lead. Not *your* leader.

You.

When you recognize this truth, you can do the work to put people first, become a leader worth following, and change the health of the organization—regardless of where you are in the hierarchy.

Heartbeat Leaders empower themselves to take charge of their career and make it their own.

Heartbeat Leaders engage their team and position them for success.

Heartbeat Leaders impact their organization for years to come.

The choice is yours. Choose to listen to the pulse of your leadership, your people, and your organization, and embrace the road ahead. Nothing gets done without people, and any problem can be solved through people.

The question is will you listen to *your* heartbeat and lead the way?

ABOUT THE AUTHOR

BestU4Life founder Dawn S. Kirk has coached, trained, and developed more than 10,000 associates in Fortune 100 companies using her Heartbeat Leadership method. She has spent over 26 years working with #1 Consumer Packaged Good companies across sales, finance, marketing, operations, national accounts, and commercial.

For sixteen of those years, she held senior executive positions with Frito-Lay, Inc. (PepsiCo) and The Coca-Cola Company, leading teams as large as 5,000 employees through organizational growth, transformations, and transitions. She has earned numerous awards, including Georgia's 100 Most Powerful and Influential Women and was inducted into the VIP Woman of the Year Circle by the National Association of Professional Women.

Dawn created BestU4Life to help corporate executives and their organizations take a People-First approach to unleash untapped potential and translate strategy into best-in-class execution. Dawn believes that people are the heartbeat of every business, and no matter what the problem is, it can be solved through people.

Dawn lives with her husband of twenty-six years, Tony Kirk, and their two teenage sons, Kendall and Kristopher, near Atlanta, Georgia. She is actively involved in her church and contributes as a member of the church board.

Visit heartbeatleadershipbook.com for leadership resources and help to ensure your leadership heart is healthy.

ACKNOWLEDGEMENTS

First, I give all Honor and Glory to Jesus Christ for the vision, resources, and strength to write this book.

Thank you also to my husband, Tony Kirk, for investing and believing in me and for the countless hours he spent reviewing drafts, listening to my ideas—and for being my biggest fan.

Thank you to my Pastors, Reverend Dr. Virgil Humes of New Hope Church in Wayne, Michigan, and Pastor Lee Jenkins of Eagles Nest Church, Alpharetta, Georgia for their spiritual instruction and for trusting me and providing me with additional opportunities to develop my leadership.

Thank you to my team at StoryBuilders—Bill Blankschaen, Akemi Cole, Ann Ferris Caston, and Jesse Barnett—for helping me bring my ideas to life and walking with me through every step of this process from idea to shelf.

Thanks to my Coach, Anthony Flynn of Amazing CEO, for pushing me out of my comfort zone to write this book and for introducing me to StoryBuilders.

Thanks to my former colleagues: Sam Wash, Rich Peterson (deceased), Mike Chapman, Terry Thomas, Glen Walter, Pam Stewart, Carolyn Jackson, and Troy Ellis for investing in my development and serving as mentors and sponsors during my Corporate Career. To my Executive Assistants—Jelani Dais, Wendy Marino, Trina DeCamp—thanks for helping me be efficient and organized throughout my executive career.

ENDNOTES

1. Galvin, Joe, et al. "CEO Optimism Falls to 8-Year Low in Q3 2019 Vistage CEO Survey." *Vistage Research Center*, 14 Jan. 2020, www.vistage.com/research-center/business-financials/economic-trends/20191003-ceo-optimism-falls-to-8-year-low-according-to-q3-2019-ceo-survey-vistage/.

2. Ncarpenter@ustravel.org. "State of American Vacation 2018." *U.S. Travel Association*, 18 Oct. 2019, www.ustravel.org/research/state-american-vacation-2018.

3. "8 Employee Engagement Statistics You Need to Know in 2020 [INFOGRAPHIC]." *The Employee Communications and Advocacy Blog*, blog.smarp.com/employee-engagement-8-statistics-you-need-to-know.

4. "Benefits of a People-First Culture." *Inc.com*, Inc., 16 Aug. 2017, www.inc.com/t-mobile/benefits-of-a-people-first-culture.html.

5. Harter, Jim. "Dismal Employee Engagement Is a Sign of Global Mismanagement." *Gallup.com*, Gallup, 27 Feb. 2020, www.gallup.com/workplace/231668/dismal-employee-engagement-sign-global-mismanagement.aspx.

6. Sheth, Shreya. *America's Top Fears 2019*. www.chapman.edu/wilkinson/research-centers/babbie-center/_files/americas-top-fears-2019.pdf.

7. Watkins, Michael. *The First 90 Days, Updated and Expanded: Proven Strategies for Getting Up to Speed Faster and Smarter.* Harvard Business Review Press, 2013.

8. Fuller, Chris. *Inspired Leadership: Your Proven Path to Remarkable Results.* Right Path Resources, 2020.

9. Maxwell, John. "9 Ways to Lead Your Leader." *John Maxwell*, 17 June 2013, www.johnmaxwell.com/blog/9-ways-to-lead-your-leader/.

10. Clear, James. *Atomic Habits: The Life-Changing Million Copy Bestseller.* Random House, 2018.